AUTONOMIC COMPASS
FINDING HOME IN YOUR NERVOUS SYSTEM

NATUREZA GABRIEL

AUTHOR OF **THE NEUROBIOLOGY OF CONNECTION**

"Gabriel has brought together some of the cutting-edge work in autonomic physiology, neurobiology and neuroscience within the broader context of late-stage capitalism. Healing in absence of context can amplify trauma. This book attempts to address the decontextualization of modern science, and in the process, engages the reader in deep neural cartography for troubled times. This work is pioneering the emerging field of what Gabriel calls connection phenomenology. It is timely and necessary."

–ALNOOR LADHA
CO-AUTHOR OF POST CAPITALIST PHILANTHROPY: HEALING WEALTH IN THE TIME OF COLLAPSE

"Neurobiology of Connection is a book we all need—a user's manual for our nervous systems. Brilliantly insightful and practical, we can learn to understand why we are the way we are moment-to-moment, meet our needs in ways that heal old traumas, and enhance deep connection with other humans and the world around us. Gabriel brings together material from indigenous cultures, neuroscience, neurochemistry, mindfulness, somatically-informed trauma work, Polyvagal Theory, and literature, combined with attention to his inner world, in order to create an updated model of the Autonomic Nervous System. I have made so many changes to the way I teach, and my students are loving it!"

–MARCIA MILLER
CERTIFIED YOGA THERAPIST, REIKI MASTER TEACHER, SENIOR TEACHER FOR UZIT

"My first nervous system health mentor introduced me to both Polyvagal Theory and the concept of 'cellular safely'. As a bodyworker practicing Visceral Manipulation through a trauma and nervous system lens, I use the sensitivity of my hands to introduce cellular safety to decontextualized stress responses (also known as tension) in the body. From the release of tension anchored in safety, systemic well-being emerges and continues to emerge as the body continues to be approached and supported in this way. It has been a challenge to find my work accurately represented through a lens of neurobiology. I am beyond grateful for this eloquent expansion of Polyvagal Theory that brings in the knowing of my hands and the wisdom that flows from our bodies to our heart, then our brain.

I also deeply appreciate Gabriel for naming the domination mindset that is imbedded into the fabric of modernity and for challenging the status quo around it. It is bold and necessary."

"Gabriel has waved a poetic wand over off-putting medical-speak and pulled the curtain back on the divine delighting herself in her magic shop. In this monumental work that is being constructed through him, I get to press my nose against that glass. I tell people the work Gabriel is conducting is the science behind safety. Bravo maestro! A Slam Dunk."

The Neurobiology of Connection is a breathing, moving testimony to the profound magic our bodies, with our autonomic nervous systems as creative center, eternally weave. This book pierces the layers of patriarchy and disembodied control that dominate much of the current scientific discourse. Gabriel's brilliant writing and insights are equally grounded in neuroscience and deep timeless inquiry, and offer the essential map to the dance of wholeness and connection we all own as birthright.

"Gabriel's work with the autonomic nervous system offers powerful keys to understanding how to participate in relational spaces that consciously nurture trusting relationships and invite creativity. These are key ingredients for the kind of ongoing attunement we need to generate a culture of care, belonging, and collective wellbeing. The neurobiology of connection is a wide open gateway to inform the awareness of human connection that is essential to create contexts for diverse people to come together and navigate the many complex, intersecting challenges we face as a species on this planet. If you recognize the importance of lived experience on our ability to form healthy relationships with ourselves and others, build community and collaborate for social and environmental change, this body of work offers an embodied, highly functional map to actively heal the fractured social territory of our times."

AUTONOMIC COMPASS

FINDING HOME IN YOUR NERVOUS SYSTEM

NATUREZA GABRIEL

AUTHOR OF THE NEUROBIOLOGY OF CONNECTION

AUTONOMIC COMPASS
NATUREZA GABRIEL

© 2025 Jaguar Imprints of Hearth Science, Inc. & Gabriel Kram

Published by:
Jaguar Imprints
PO Box 567, Nicasio, CA 94946, USA

A CIP record for this book is available from the Library of Congress Cataloging-in-Publication Data

Printed in USA

TABLE OF CONTENTS

01- INTRODUCTION

Have you ever learned something that changed your life the moment you understood it?

I remember having this happen as a small child. Sometimes learning something, like that the earth was revolving around the Sun, or that dinosaurs roamed the earth aeons of time before us, change your experience of the world *around* you, literally altering your picture of the Universe and your place in it. To realize that the earth is actually located on the arm of a giant starry pinwheel, in one of numberless galaxies, revolving around a star, cannot help but change your experience of *where* we are located. To realize that the same ground you are walking on has been tread by alien reptile beings who existed so long ago that the timespans are incomprehensible, changes your experience of *when* we are located.

Sometimes, on the other hand, you learn something that changes not your experience of the world *around* you, but your experience of the world *inside* you. These experiences tend to take place not in how you see or imagine the world, not in your head where you think, but in your body. In how it *feels* to be you. They slow your heart down or speed it up, change your breathing, evoke a wave of emotion. Something shifts or changes, mysterious levers move and grind internally, and you find yourself different inwardly. Sometimes in ways that do not shift back.

The strongest inward pivot of my young life was being taken away from the tiny rural town in New Hampshire where I grew up. It happened when I was seven years old, in 1982. My father lost a job, and my parents, who had a young family, packed our lives into boxes, put them into a yellow Ryder truck, and drove us across the country, away from everyone and every place I knew or cared about.

My brother is four and a half years younger than I am, so he was only three years old when this happened. He doesn't remember it. If I were a different kid with a different constitution–if I hadn't fallen so deeply in love with that place that it lived totally inside my skin– perhaps that experience would not have wrecked me. But it did. I could not get over it.

Many decades later I would read William Maxwell's painfully beautiful autobiography *So Long, See You Tomorrow*. The book was written when the author was seventy-two, reflecting in part on the loss of his mother sixty years before. In one of the climactic scenes near the end of the book, the author, who is the narrator, finds himself in the office of a psycho-analyst in New York City, and realizes that when he has tried to say, about this loss, that he could not bear it, what has come out of his mouth is, "I cannot bear it." He is simply unable to speak it in the past tense. The loss is not behind him, in the past. It is in every moment of his present. The scene ends with him weeping inconsolably, unable to stop, walking into Central Park.

Not only could I not get over it– the experience smoldered so painfully with loss that I could not approach it inwardly at all. Like a radioactive site cordoned off for the safety of the community, I could not get anywhere near the loss. The grief was so consuming that all I could do was try to get away from it, an inward accident I could distract myself from during the day, but that turned with sleep into night terrors so severe for months that my parents had to hold me down for fear I would injure myself.

What my parents took me away from– and mind you, I am not suggesting that they should not have done this, I am not blaming them amymore– was so deeply written into my heart that it was as though they nearly ripped my heart itself out. They had been part of a tight-knit community, I had there a best friend I have known since he was five days old (that's him in

both pictures on the previous page- in the top one he is facing away from the camera, I am to the right, in the bottom one he is sitting closer to the camera in the boat. His stepfather is the man in both pictures.) I had had a second mother, pictured at right in the upper photo: his mom. What I had experienced in the heart of the deep New England forests, the flinty water, the warmth of woodburning stoves in snowdrifted winter, the running of sap in the Maples, the call of frogs, and the closeness of our village was a sense of belonging so deep, so primal, so natural, so complete, and so mysterious that I thought it was simply who I was. I belonged to that place and those people. It was simple as that.

The shock of being taken away from this was one from which I did not truly recover until December 15, 2023. If you do the calculations– I left New Hampshire in November 1982, I recovered from leaving in December 2023, you will realize that the timespan between these two events is forty-one years. December 15, 2023 was the day that I closed on a ten-acre forested property in Northern California that carries the same primal vibrations of wilderness present in the place I grew up. At around 2 pm, on the day that the seller accepted our offer, I was walking on the property when I got a call from our real estate agent. *Congratulations*, she said.

I was facing our film studio in a three-acre meadow ringed by old-growth Douglas fir trees. The moment she said this, without my body moving at all– I was just standing there holding the phone up to my ear– something cracked back into place in my chest so loudly (the relocation sounded like a wishbone being snapped) that I asked her on the phone if she had heard it. I have no idea anatomically what that was, but I also know with the same certainty I know that I am breathing that it was my whole heart coming back into joint.

It took me forty-one years to find my way fully back home. That moment marked the culmination of a forty-one year odyssey, and it is also the reason that I wrote this book, and the reason that I write all my books. All of the work that I do is about finding home in a human nervous system.

What I would like to do here, in *Autonomic Compass,* is distill down thirty years of what I have learned about the deepest layers of our neurology, what it means, and why it matters to your life into the briefest volume possible. This is not really a narrative: it is not even a story. It is a navigational instrument. An inward compass.

Hello. I'm Gabriel, the one writing this for you. I've spent nearly thirty years studying the nervous system and mindful awareness, with the last fifteen focused almost exclusively on the Autonomic Nervous System. I studied at Yale and Stanford Universities, and I've been mentored by a dozen of the world's leading experts in connection science and wellbeing, as well as over a hundred advisors from 25 disciplines of wellbeing in 24 cultures. I founded and lead a global wellness firm that has created the world's most accurate neural cartographies of these systems, and I have written ten books on the art and science of connection. Yet the reason I do all of these things is because of what happened to me as a child, and what it took to heal from that. I want to help you find your way home if I can. I don't want it to take you forty-one years.

I am a father, a husband, a forest tender, and a person con-cerned about human and planetary flourishing. I am interested in seeing a global shift in how modern humans inhabit their deep nervous systems because this leads to the most rapid change in how people feel and therefore behave. What you are reading is a practical handbook to demystify your Autonomic Nervous System, which is the biological system with the stron-gest shaping force over your health. Strangely, most humans know very little about it. I would like to change that. I believe that learning autonomic fluency is one of the most potent ways you can improve your life. And you can learn it right here, right now, over the next 150 pages. If you allow it to, it may change the *where*, the *when*, the *how*, and the *who* you understand yourself to be.

Before we begin, I'd like to give you a sense of some of my limitations here as your guide, and to whom I am speaking in this volume.

In this book

I WILL ASSUME THE BASIC MENTAL HEALTH OF THE READER

If you are actively psychotic, have an Axis One or Two disorder, or are suffering from a debilitating mental health condition, some of what I am recommending may be harmful or not possible.

I AM NOT ADEQUATELY TRAINED TO MEET THE NEEDS OF A NEURODIVERGENT POPULATION

If you have the sense that you are neuro-divergent, and are part of communities that view the world through this lens (e.g., the greater Autism community), I am simply not educated well enough about this perspective to guarantee my usefulness in your learning journey. Take what I am saying with a grain of salt; examine it in trusted community; take what is useful & discard the rest. Please let us know if we can improve this text to better align with your experience or better meet your needs.

I AM NOT ADEQUATELY TRAINED TO MEET THE NEEDS OF AN LGBTQ+ OR TRANS POPULATION

I confess that my experience of gender, and gender expression may blind or impair my ability to perceive certain aspects of the LGBTQ+ experience, or the trans experience, that render my observations inaccurate or unhelpful for this population. If this is your experience, please do not take my observations at face value, but examine them within a trusted community. Please let us know if we can improve this text to better align with your experience or better meet your needs.

I AM NOT ADEQUATELY TRAINED TO MEET THE NEEDS OF PEOPLE OF CULTURE, INDIGENOUS PEOPLE, OR WOMEN

Having been acculturated in the United States, and growing up in a body that was acculturated as white, straight, and male, the body I am wearing carries structural privileges of which I am, despite having done a lot of 'work' on myself, not fully aware. This may cause alterations or biases or deficencies in my worldview that render my observations for non-white or non-male readers to be inaccurate or unhelpful. If this is your experience, please do not take my observations at face value, but examine them within a trusted community. Please let us know if we can improve this text to better align with your experience or better meet your needs.

I WILL ASSUME THAT YOU ARE NOT SEVERELY CHRONICALLY ILL

Although this book will be relevant for you, there are feedback loops active in chronic illness that may require a) some alteration in methodologies, b) additional inputs or modifications, c) additional variables to address these feedbacks that are beyond the scope of this text. These eventualities are addressed in my book *Autonomics for Chronic Illness*.

I WILL ASSUME THAT YOU DO NOT HAVE A NEURO-DEGENERATIVE DISEASE

As in complex chronic illness, there are methodological modifications required to the scope of this work that are beyond the current text.

I WILL ASSUME THAT YOU ARE TRAUMATIZED

If you have grown up in 'modern civilization', you are traumatized.

My mentor Vincent Felitti, MD, Co-Principal Investigator of the ACES (Adverse Chilhood Experiences) study identified ten categories of early childhood adversity, and discovered that in a patient population of middle class adults at a private health insurance provider, 67% of them had at least one early childhood adverse experience. Felitti's groundbreaking study, done at Kaiser Permanente in the 1990s, helped educate the general population about the prevalence of trauma in the general population. Prior to his study, the general concept was that trauma was confined to veterans returning from service, and a few unfortunate others who had been abused. My mentor Nadine Burke Harris MD MPH, the former first Surgeon General of California, brought Felitti's study proactively into the domain of public health through the ACES Aware Initiative in California.

Yet Felitti's study failed to account for any sort of sociological trauma–sexism, racism, homophobia, or any discrimination based on creed, class, or geography. To his original category, we could therefore easily add seven categories of sociological trauma. The study did not even conceive of alienation from the Living World as a category of early adversity, yet our deep ancestral baseline requires this as a native input. If you added these additional categories, the only people alive today who are not traumatized would be uncontacted tribes living in small band hunter gatherer configurations, which account for less than one tenth of one percent of all people currently alive on earth.

Unless you have found this book lying on a rock in the middle of indigenous territory in the Amazon basin, and that is where you are from ancestrally, and that is where you grew up, and you've never seen or dealt with the incursions of the modern world, and somehow you can read this– if you are reading this book you are traumatized.

Now I would like to clarify my role as your guide.

I AM NOT A THERAPIST

I do not think like a therapist, or act like a therapist. Possibly I look like a therapist, you can decide if you see me. Certainly I have some sweaters that look like they would be very much at home in the wardrobe of a therapist.

THINK OF ME AS A SENSEI

You will have more success with this project if you understand that I am basically running a dojo. I am working to train you. And so

- You can ignore anything I am saying, and that is fine
- I understand my job as being to wake people up
- You may not like what I am saying at times
- I don't mind that you may not like what I am saying

I'M GONNA WRITE LIKE WE ARE HAVING A CONVERSATION

Welcome to *Autonomic Compass*. This is a practical handbook designed to familiarize you with the workings of your Autonomic Nervous System.

While each of us has one, yours has been uniquely shaped by your history, life experience, circumstances growing up, the body you are wearing, the culture you are part of, and your interactions with the Living World.

What I'm going to teach are simple principles: what I want you to do is figure out how they apply specifically to you, and how you can get home to yourself. Thanks for joining me. I'm glad you are here. Please keep a writing instrument with you as you read, and mark this thing up. One final note: I'm going to abbreviate the Autonomic Nervous System as the ANS.

02- AILMENTS & ISSUES WITH A SIGNIFICANT AUTONOMIC COMPONENT

Adverse Childhood Experiences
Anxiety
Attachment Issues
Autism
Auto-Immune Illness
Cancer
Chronic Illness
Complex Regional Pain Syndrome
Depression
Developmental Trauma
Frozen Shoulder
Gastro-Intestinal Distress
Grief
Heart Disease
Inability to Gain Weight
Inability to Lose Weight
Inflammatory Bowel Disease (IBD)
Mast Cell Activation Syndrome
Migraines
Neurodiversity
Parkinson's Disease
Performance Anxiety
PTSI: Post-Traumatic Stress Injury: it's not a Disorder
Racism
Sexism
Sleep Disorders
Stress (Chronic, Toxic, and Traumatic)
Ulcerative Colitis

03- DINNER IS SERVED

This book is like a nice home-cooked meal.

Your friends are gathered around a farm table in front of a fireplace. You are at ease. The food is delicious. Nourishing. Unfussy.

The book is not long, but like a nutritious meal, I want to invite you to really digest what I'm saying here. Give yourself time to absorb it. Linger over it and take your time.

Because it could totally change your life.

I'm going to teach you something that we call autonomic fluency. Autonomic, because it's about your autonomic nervous system. Fluency because in the same way that you speak your native language without having to think about it, I want you to be fluent in how your autonomic nervous system shapes your moment-to-moment experience.

Your autonomic nervous system is the deepest layer of your neurology. Think of it like bedrock. It is your deepest neurological geology. It's way down beneath language, and culture. Its programming is the primal language of survival. It tunes your body and mind, depending on whether you feel safe, in danger, or under life threat.

This tuning, what we will call 'autonomic state', controls the deepest and most powerful levers that govern your moment-to-moment experience of wellbeing.

From this tuning, your body is either able to enter connection states, which are health creating– or gets pulled into defensive states, which are disease creating.

Every single response you ever have to stress will be mediated by this system. Doesn't matter whether your are stressed about homework, or money, or your partner. Doesn't matter whether you are stressed about your health or politics. Doesn't matter whether you are stressed because of the climate, or robots, or being deported. Literally every single time that your body finds itself in danger or under lifethreat, it will be governed by this system.

Furthermore, your thriving is governed by this system. Every single time that you are feeling well in your life, from organic causes, it will be because this system is functioning smoothly.

Learn the language of these systems and you move from being a passenger to sitting in the driver's seat of your health. Learn the language of these systems and you move from awareness, to fluency, to agency over your trajectory. Learn the language of these systems and you are learning an original language of Life. Learn the language of these systems and you can steer your life in the direction of home.

AS THOUGH IT WERE A DELICIOUS MEAL, REALLY DIGEST THIS BOOK. IT COULD TOTALLY CHANGE YOUR LIFE.

04- WHAT IS TRAUMA?

I have studied, and been personally and professionally involved in the transformation of trauma for the past twenty years, yet I am increasingly uncomfortable with this ambiguous word, and increasingly aware that what it means in the culture at large, and what it means to me as someone working in the field of trauma transformation, are different. I would like to frame a conversation around trauma that feels more practically useful.

THE ACES STUDY

In 1998, Vincent Felitti MD conducted the Adverse Childhood Experiences Study (ACES) at Kaiser Permanente in San Diego. The study, which grew to include 17,337 adult patients at a private pay health insurer, would demonstrate that 67% of a college-educated population had one or more ACES. The study demonstrated a graded dose-response relationship between early adversity and adverse health outcomes later in life. In plain language, the more early adversity you have of whatever kind, if this is not treated at its roots, the worse your health will be over your entire lifespan. These lifespan health outcomes, evident 50 years after the inciting events, span physical health impacts, mental health impacts, and substance abuse. A person with 4 of more ACES is up to 12X more likely to develop anxiety, depression, suicidality, heart disease, cancer, diabetes, and lung disease, or to struggle with alcohol and drug abuse.

LIMITATIONS OF THE ACES STUDY

While Felitti's study brought to the mainstream population an awareness of the prevalence of early adversity– the enduring impacts from growing up with abuse and neglect[1] and

---

1   The study addressed ten categories of early adversity, including: Physical abuse, Sexual abuse, Emotional abuse, Physical neglect, Emotional neglect, Witnessing domestic violence, Substance abuse in

the reality that at least two-thirds of the adult population was experiencing the adverse health outcomes resulting from it– the study failed to acknowledge many categories of adversity the inclusion of which would have substantively broadened our sense of who is suffering traumatic impacts. Broadly, the study failed to conceive of ACES resulting from sociological phenomena (sexism, racism, homophobia, religious persecution, etc.), as well as not accounting for ACES resulting from alienation from the Living World. The inclusion of these two broad categories (social and ecological ACES) would have brought the modern population's exposure to trauma up to 100%.

Furthermore, it was beyond Felitti's purview to describe the mechanisms of trauma. Events were traumatizing to people as evidenced by the degree to which they compromised health outcomes later in life, across physical and mental health domains, but articulating the neurobiological mechanisms of trauma was outside of the study's scope.

What Felitti did note, and which in itself is a stunning realization, was that simply creating a context where a patient could talk about early adversity with their physician (in the wake of the administration of the screening, the patient would be informed that they had an ACES score and invited to share anything with their doctor that they thought could help the physician better treat them), had a profoundly positive effect on people's health. Simply acknowledging early adversity, in the presence of a non-judgemental health professional, was profoundly alleviating to symptoms. [2] The potency of this observation is enormous, because what it means is that allowing the conscious mind (ordinary sense of self) to acknowledge what the body knows (as opposed to keeping this knowledge seques-

---

the household, Mental illness in the household, Parental separation or divorce, Loss of a parent through death or abandonment

2   When Kaiser implemented a data science model to track the utilization of services in the wake of implementing the ACES screening, they discovered that patient utilization of outpatient services had dropped dramatically, saving the system $2 billion annually. (Notes, Felitti, interview and personal correspondence February 2021)

tered outside of conscious awareness) is transformational.

Felitti recognized, and he spoke to this extensively when I interviewed him, that, *What we are often treating in public health as the disease* [e.g., the behavior that brings someone into care] *is the patient's solution to a deeper problem that we cannot see.* This is a radical awareness, and it totally reframes our understanding of behavior. Through this lens we recognize that smoking, or over-eating, or self-medicating with cocaine, amphetamines, alcohol, heroine– is not actually the problem. It is *the best solution that the patient has found* to addressing an underlying problem that we cannot see.

When we then treat someone in a smoking cessation program, we are removing their best solution, not treating their underlying problem. If we do not recognize this, the program will fail to achieve its desired outcome, because the person is not addicted to nicotine because they like cigarettes. They are addicted to nicotine because although costly (smoking will kill you), it successfully medicates an underlying condition (nicotine has marvelous anti-anxiety properties). It stands to reason that if we could effectively address the problem we cannot see (underlying ANS dysregulation creating anxiety), the solution they have chosen might not be necessary any longer (you don't bother to self-medicate a problem you no longer have). The same logic applies to pretty much any kind of addiction. And what is the problem that we cannot see? Now we are getting closer to a definition of trauma.

The problem that we cannot see is the deflection of the Autonomic Nervous System from its ancestral baseline in safety and connection. It turns out that the human species has an ancestral baseline in safety and connection: an evolved nest that creates the foundation of our ability to thrive. A certain set of neurological inputs that we need in order to maintain wellbeing.

The problem is that in the wake of some event, or some series of events, we no longer feel *safe*. And now we are getting at the heart of it, because human thriving only happens when our nervous systems reside in their ancestral baseline of safety and connection.

Having focused for nearly the past twenty years on mapping the physiology and energy-processing templates of the autonomic nervous system, I can also tell you that trauma is not a one-size-fits-all phenomenon, because its presence and symptomology is a distinct result of the precise manner in which the ANS has been deflected from its baseline. The particular ways in which a person does not feel good is a map of the way that the ANS has been shifted away from its ancestral baseline.

The specific way in which trauma manifests– be it as chronic anxiety, depression, heart disease, auto-immune illness, sleep difficulties, or relational challenges is a result of the manner in which the ANS has been deflected from our ancestral baseline of thriving, and in order to understand this for yourself, you will need to develop autonomic fluency.

Furthermore, being deviated from safety and connection compounds upon itself, because human wellbeing is social in nature, and when we do not feel safe we are not inclined to be social. This explains why, in May of 2023, Vivek Murthy, the Surgeon General of the United States, issued a Surgeon General's Advisory on the epidemic of loneliness. Loneliness is one of the root drivers of mental distress, is contributory to mental illness, and has the same effects on longevity as smoking 15 cigarettes per day.

Most modern people are lonely. The Cigna Loneliness Index indicates that prior to the COVID-19 pandemic 49% of American adults were lonely, and during the pandemic this figure rose to 60%. That is 3 out of 5 people.
We are lonely, isolated, and disconnected for the simple reason that modern people do not feel safe in our bodies.

If we do not feel safe, we do not activate the biology of connection. If we do not activate the biology of connection, the biology of defense does not turn off. When defense becomes our normal state we become ill. Sometimes the illness is primarily physical, sometimes it is primarily mental. Sometimes illness happens quickly, sometimes slowly. But it happens every single time.

The part of us that determines whether we live in defense because we do not feel safe enough, or we open into connection because we do is the Autonomic Nervous System.

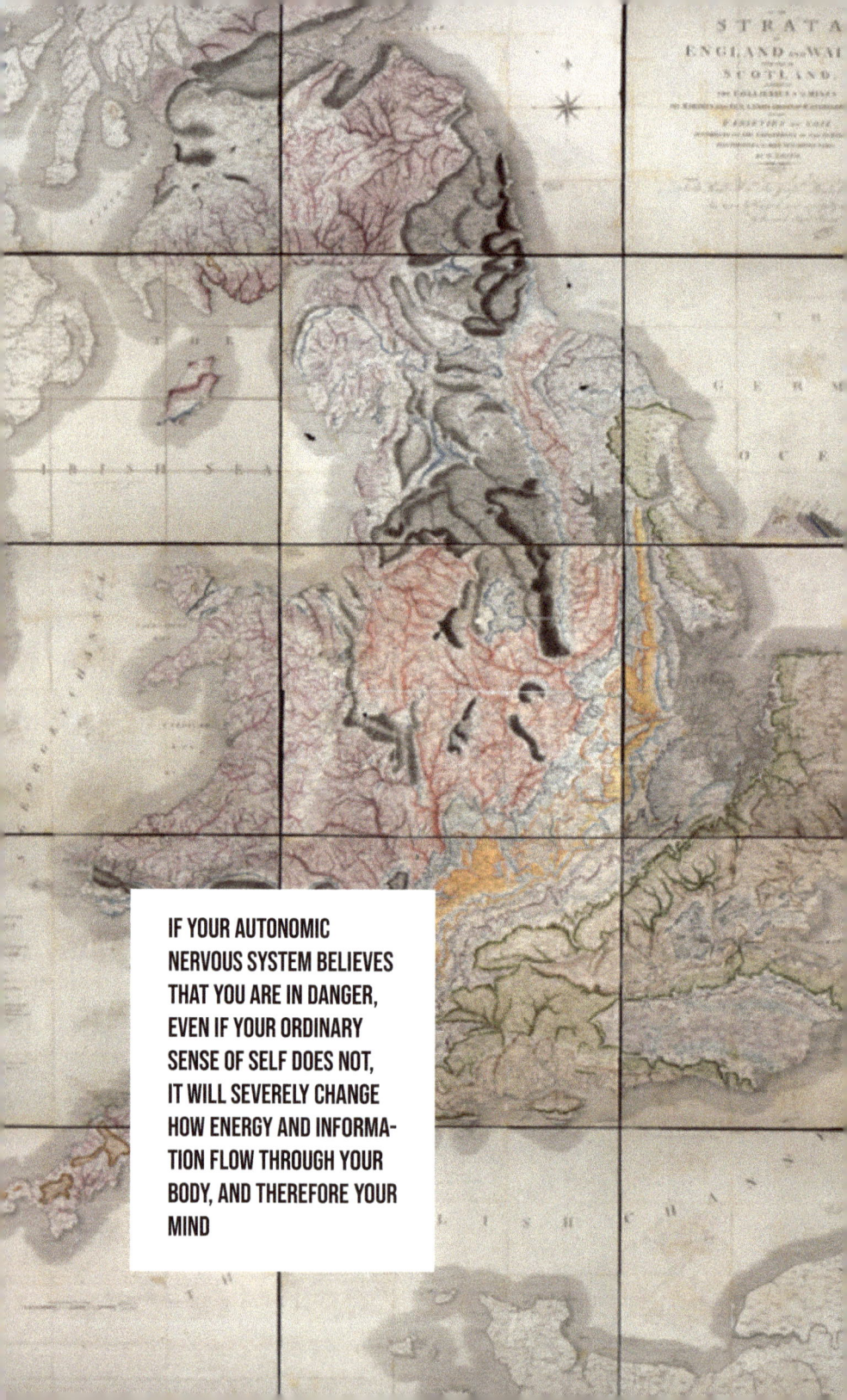

IF YOUR AUTONOMIC NERVOUS SYSTEM BELIEVES THAT YOU ARE IN DANGER, EVEN IF YOUR ORDINARY SENSE OF SELF DOES NOT, IT WILL SEVERELY CHANGE HOW ENERGY AND INFORMATION FLOW THROUGH YOUR BODY, AND THEREFORE YOUR MIND

05- THE MAP THAT CHANGED THE WORLD

I first began to really pay attention to the autonomic nervous system fifteen years ago. I was studying trauma healing. And Twig Wheeler[1], who was teaching us, began talking about a geological map from 1815 created by a man named William Smith. It is known as 'the map that changed the world.' It is pictured at left. If you look closely, in the upper right corner, it says, *A Delineation of the Strata of England and Wales with Part of Scotland.*

Strata are layers. You are looking at the first geologic map of England and Wales: the deep layers of the earth. Way down beneath the surface. What Twig explained to us is that **the Autonomic Nervous System is the deepest geologic layer of the nervous system.** It is universal, far beneath language, beneath culture. Your deepest neurological strata.

The Autonomic Nervous System has two functions. First, it is responsible for maintaining the *internal milieu.* I'm using the French word here, because this is how it is talked about by health professionals. *Homeostasis,* or *homeostatic balance* are other words used for this: maintaining the inner workings of your body in dynamic balance. All the things that you don't have to think about. Unlike, say, moving your arm to pick up a glass of water, the autonomic nervous system beats your heart, breathes your lungs, pulses your digestion, dilates your pupils, contracts your blood vessels...all without you *doing* anything. You don't have to tell it to take care of any of this stuff; it does it automatically. For this reason, you can think of it as the ***Automatic*** *Nervous System.*

---

1 Anthony 'Twig' Wheeler is a self-described Cultural Animator. He was teaching me as part of a three-year Somatic Experiencing® training: the naturalistic approach to the resolution of trauma developed by Peter Levine, PhD.

Secondly, and this is really important and unknown to most people: it shapes the banks of the river of energy flowing through you. It literally dials up and down the master control switches that govern how your body responds to your inner and outer environment. Both of these functions relate to survival.

And if your Autonomic Nervous System believes that you are in danger, even if your ordinary sense of self does not, it will severely change how energy and information flow through your body, and therefore your mind. Like glasses you cannot take off, it will change how everything feels and appears inwardly and outwardly in a split second.

I've spent the past fifteen years rigorously studying the geology of this deep nervous system with well over a hundred advisors. The company I lead has created the world's most accurate map of it. And learning to read that map is going to improve your life *a lot* because it will give you direct contact with the part of your nervous system that is driving the most fundamental systems that govern your moment-to-moment experience of wellbeing. Literally every system in your body is downstream of the Autonomic Nervous System. I cannot think of a single system that is not.

From the way your digestion and immune system work, to how hard your heart is beating, how deeply you are breathing, how clearly you are thinking, how accurately you are perceiving your inner and outer environment, how your attention works, to how your muscles respond, to your sense of balance— all of the inner workings of your body are downstream of your autonomic assessments of safety, danger, and lifethreat. It governs the master levers, slides, and dials that control how you experience everything that flows through you.

AUTONOMIC PRESETS CONTROL THE WAY IT FEELS TO BE IN YOUR BODY, HOW YOU EXPERIENCE YOURSELF, THE EMOTIONS AVAILABLE TO YOU, THE KIND OF THOUGHTS THAT YOU THINK, THE WAY THAT YOU PERCEIVED THE WORLD AROUND YOU, THE WAY YOU BEHAVE.

06- MASTER LEVERS

Have you ever been to a recording studio? Or if not, have you ever owned a stereo or a boombox with a graphic equalizer on it? You know, one of those sets of sliders where you could push the bass all the way up to make it bump, or tweak the treble so that opera arias shatter glass? Your autonomic nervous system runs the master sliders that govern your moment-to-moment experience of well-being.

Its presets control the way it feels to be in your body, how you experience yourself, the emotions available to you, the kind of thoughts you think, the way that you perceive the world around you, and the way you behave. Learning autonomic fluency is a way of taking charge so that you can grasp and move these deepest levers that govern your well-being.

Your Autonomic Nervous System, you see, comes with a number of tuning presets.

In the same way that you can adjust a graphic equalizer preset to give you the epic surround sound of a Stadium Rock Concert, or the intimacy of a tiny Jazz Club, your Autonomic Nervous System comes with a set of standard presets that shape the river of energy and experience flowing through you.

Once you understand how they work, and can identify the presets that are active, you can learn to change the inputs to your **neuroception, neurology,** and **neurochemistry** to get unstuck from maladaptive states, and actively increase your health. (Don't worry, I'm going to explain each of those terms.)

It's something you can learn to do in any moment of your life for free. You don't need a wi-fi signal or an app, or a special ring, or to attach an electrode, or a thermometer, or to take some drug. It's pretty simple, and there are no side effects.

07- YOUR BODY IS THE SITE OF THIS EXPERIMENT

Your Autonomic Nervous System is the neural architecture of your bodymind connection. Lots of people call your system a mind-body system, but in the United States, when we say 'mind' most people think *brain*, so that mind-body sounds like brain-body. And this puts the emphasis in the wrong place. The emphasis needs to go on body. So, *body*mind.

Most of the actual neural wiring of the Autonomic Nervous System is not in your brain, but in your body. About eighty percent (4 out of 5) of its fibers are sending information from receptors in the body (your skin, your organs, your inward sensing of limbs, etc.) inward to your deeper nervous system and upward to your brain. Modern neuroscience has gotten really fixated on the brain in your head, but your body is jam-packed with brains. Let me say that differently. If the brain that you think of as your brain is neurology that processes information, this information processing system is distributed in the body far more broadly than neuroscience lets on, and way more broadly than most of us realize.

A significant amount of this processing happens at neural junctions, which are neural clusters technically called *ganglia*, which in turn aggregate into *plexes*. Ganglia are typically clusters of five to ten thousand interneurons that might contain millions to billions of synaptic connections. They are capable of localized decision-making. When they aggregate into a plexus there can be many more neurons and exponentially more connections. There are twenty-three pairs of ganglia running up and down your spine, and there are ten plexes in the body[1]. That

---

1 According to orthodox neurology, which might be wrong about this, on the 'sympathetic' side there are three cervical ganglia, 12 thoracic ganglia, four lumbar ganglia, and four or five sacral ganglia. There are four 'parasympathetic' ganglia in the head: the ciliary,

makes fifty-six brains outside of the brain in your head.

This does not include the intrinsic brain of the heart, which contains more neural cells than muscle cells. This does not include the enteric brain of the guts, which is the place from which gut feelings originate. [2]

So by my best reckoning the body contains fifty-nine brains, including that in your head. This is probably not true. The number is probably *far greater*. I say this with some degree of confidence, because orthodox neurology is so deeply wrong about so much of what it tells you about your nervous system. It is so wrong that on holidays what I like to do is escstatically dance on the dessicated bones of orthodox neuroscience until I pulverize them into powder. (Everyone needs a hobby, right?)

Thinking of your body as having 59 brains, while it could be an amusing thing to tell people at a party, is also not super-useful because your entire body is so profoundly infused with neurology that effectively your entire body is your brain. The reason most people do not understand this, including most medical professionals, is because neurological dissections are done on cadavers. And in the same way that a tree, when it dies, loses its leaves, the body, when it dies, loses the finest branching divisions of its neurology. All of the medical textbooks in the world are based on diagrams of neurology that came from dead people.

Because we have been taught to believe what our eyes are telling us, because most of the early anatomists (I'm talking 17th - 19th century) who built the foundation maps that have informed the development of modern neurology identified with

---

otic, pterygopalatine, and submandibular ganglia. As for the ten plexes, those would be the Spinal: Cervical, brachial, lumbar, sacral, and coccygeal. And the autonomic: Celiac, Auerbachs, pharyngeal, cardiac, and Meissner's.

2 The enteric brain is subtended by a number of plexes, including the Auerbach and Meissner's, yet also contains differentiated dedicated sub-diaphragmatic vagal architecture.

thinking (*I think, therefore I am*), and because thinking happens in words and pictures in the head (cranial brain), the anatomists whose maps inform modern neuroscience were made by people who believed

1. the neural structures of significance in the body are in the cranial brain

2. the neurology of corpses is the same neurology as that of living people

3. the way a neural system looks corresponds to what it does (anatomy is the same as physiology)

4. the bigger a neurological structure is the more important it is

5. it is not necessary to map receptors to understand neurological systems

Of the five statements above, which underpin the entire foundation of orthodox neurology, exactly zero are correct. The result of these foundation errors in neurology, which set the initial conditions in which the discipline developed, are that most people think of their nervous systems as looking more or less like the tree on the following page. A trunk that divides into large branches, which sub-divide into smaller branches, and so on.

This is a diagram of either an Oak in winter, or what allopathic medicine believes your vagus nerve looks like. You decide. This is what orthodox neurology teaches. The level of detail, by which I mean specifically how far its branches divide smaller and smaller, is greater than most of what is illustrated in anatomy books.

OAK IN WINTER OR VAGUS NERVE?

Most modern people have the impression that inside of their body, there are some biological telephone wires running down from the brain, wiring all the internal organs into conversation with your brain, linking up your systems. What people utterly fail to understand is the density of the weave of living neurology woven through every part of your body.

Your skin, for example, has nine meters of c-tactile fibers per square inch. This means that there are 24,500 meters of c-tactile fiber in a human adult. C-tactile fibers are autonomic fibers, part of the autonomic nervous system, that subtend a broad range of sensory receptor types embedded in your skin. These fibers are extremely tiny. Much narrower than a human hair. Your skin is embedded with a hyper-fine mesh of them. You know how sheets are rated in terms of threadcount? 300 thread count means that there are 150 vertical, and 150 horizontal threads per square inch. If you hold such a sheet up to your face, you will barely be able to see the threads.

If the density of your c-tacticle fibers was a threadcount, your skin would be 7000 threadcount. 3500 fibers running vertically, 3500 running horizontally. (Your skin isn't woven, so this is not a perfect analogy, but visualize this.)

It has 10X the thread density of finely woven sheets. And this is just your skin. Because the autonomic nervous system is responsible for monitoring the entire interior of the body, it has corresponding density of weave inwardly.

We are very much like moving trees. And the living neurological reality of your body is that it much more closely resembles the Oak tree in summer than the Oak tree in winter. If you want to understand your living neurology, think about it like this. Your neurology is like an oak tree at the height of summer, not the winter-bare tree you have been taught to believe it is.

Most of your living neurology is not in your brain, contrary to what modern neuroscience would have you believe. Because

most of your living neurology is sensory. The very powerful and important thing this means is that if you want to alter the inputs to your nervous system, you do not have to invade the brain. You can do the same thing much more elegantly by globally changing the inputs to the Autonomic Nervous System *in the body*. Rapidly globally changing the skin temperature, for example, as happens when you throw cold water on your face, or take a cold shower, or jump in an ice bath, immediately changes the inputs to your vagus globally.

What this means practically for you, as we are starting out, is that your body is the location where most of this experiment in autonomic fluency will take place. Your body is not merely an appendage that exists to drag around your head. On the contrary, the body that you are wearing, and learning how to occupy it in an embodied manner, is the doorway to your thriving.

For some of you this will be good news, for others not so much. It depends on your relationship with your body. But that is why, at the outset, I'm explaining this. This work that you will do in autonomics will take place, its primary site of learning, will be in your body. And so you want to cultivate a particular quality of relationship with your body so that this can be useful. It is helpful to begin to regard it as the site of much deeper intelligence than most of us realize.

Let's take a look at some of the common obstacles to this deepened relationship, and how to overcome them.

I THINK THEREFORE I AM

We have been trained, in the modern world, to identify with thinking. If we track back to the origin of this tendency, it was initially an assertion of rationality in a world governed by faith, that has transfomed into an identification of identity with cognition and cognitive process. Yet the reason people reside in thinking is because we are traumatized. When people are traumatized, living in the body doesn't feel very good. If we can figure out how to wear our bodies in a way that is more nourishing, and where we feel safer, this can change.

I AM SPIRITUAL, AND THE BODY IS THEREFORE...

Irrelevant? A distraction? Sinful? There is a deep history in modern Judeo-Christian religion, in many of its variants, of dividing the body from the spirit. There are strong taboos in many religions against experiencing embodied pleasure. There are origin stories that teach than the body is sinful. Without going into all of that here, the Autonomic Nervous System is the altar of your spirit. It is a neuro-electrical interface between spirit and matter.

If you bring a body-negating spiritual stance to this work it will prevent you from working with the information, memory, and experience encoded in your nervous system, which is necessary for spiritual evolution. If the problem is the materiality of the body, rest assured that does not apply. Because your nervous system is a closed electrical system in contact proximity with a liquid pressure system connected to an oscillator called your heart, and together they create an electro-magnetic field that is detectable by a magnetometer eight feet away from you. So what we are talking about is not matter, but rather energy. This is actually a quantum light body, and the last time I checked spirituality told you to attend to your light body. That is also known as *your spirit*. Am I wrong? Tell me I'm wrong. I dare you. Doing this work will enhance your spiritual development, and yes, this work happens in the body. Most of the people who go around telling me that the body is sinful are the same people who are doing things with the body that are unethical. So instead of generalizing, perhaps they might say that their particular bodies are sinful. To which I would reply, *Then stop doing that!*

MY BODY DOESN'T FEEL GOOD

We know. That's why you are here.

I DON'T LIKE THE WAY MY BODY LOOKS

Somehow we have been taught to compare our appearance with others. I believe we are the only creatures who do this. I cannot fathom a dog thinking it wants to look more like a different dog. Or a tree thinking it wants to look like a different tree. Strangely though, learning to embrace your body as it is makes you more beautiful.

I AM AFRAID TO FEEL WHAT I AM FEELING IN MY BODY

This is because your body knows things that your mind cannot know in a language your mind does not speak. It knows things about what has happened to you, and what has happened to us, that are unspeakable. That if uttered out loud, if said in the streets, if spoken with clarity at meetings, and at family gatherings, would upset the entire apple cart of human relations. Would rupture relationships, upend marriages, cause family fueds, societal upheaval, etc. Exactly. And this is why you need to do this work. Because this is why your body doesn't feel good. This leads us then to the first foundation principle of this work, which can be summarized as follows:

Your body is the site of inquiry and experiment.

Your body is the place where you will get to know your Autonomic Nervous System. Time to make friends with her.[3]

---

3   I am gendering body female not because you, dear reader, are necessarily a woman, but because the alternative in English is to call the body 'it'. It, you will notice, is a blunt pronoun that pushes us away from the body. In English, unlike the Romance languages, proper nouns do not have gender. In French or Italian, the table is gendered feminine, so you talk about *her*. This is the semantic effect I am going for. If you are a dude reading this, the sentence could say– *Time to make friends with him.*

PRACTICE: BEFRIENDING THE BODY

Throughout the book there will be exercises for you to practice, offset like this page. Practice is crucial to this learning process. It's fine to read the book through and come back for the practices, but if you don't do the practices, you are leaving most of the food on the table. If you are using this book in the context of therapeutic or coaching work, the practices are the SKILLS that you want to build, so do not forget them!

All of us are wearing a body, but not all of us have a great relationship with our bodies. Maybe we don't like the way our bodies look, how they perform, or something else about them. Most of us do not consider that we have the ability to transform our relationship with our bodies. Sometimes this begins with how we perceive them. Realizing the degree to which our bodies are intelligent and sensitive can be helpful here. So can realizing that often the things that we don't like about our bodies are a result of chilhood adversity. If you don't feel positively toward your body, ask yourself– *when did this begin? Have I always felt this way? What happened to my relationship with my body? When did I begin treating it poorly?*

Ask your body– how you can repair this relationship? Make it a practice to recall moments when you have been grateful to your body...if you want to feel grateful for having hands, something most of us take for granted almost all of the time, go watch *Edward Scissorhands.* The entire film is about the pain of not being able to touch someone you love. What moments have you been grateful for the simple ability to touch? To move? To feel? To see? To hear? To smell? To taste? Can you feel that gratitude? When was the last time you thanked your body?

08- THE FLASHLIGHT OF ATTENTION

I'm not going to spend much time addressing it in this book, because there are many good places to learn mindful awareness these days, but the training of attention is pre-requisite to everything we are doing here. Learning to steady the mind, to point it at some aspect of the inner or outer world, to govern the beam of it so that it doesn't shake, is a foundation skill that will support everything we are doing in this book.

A good part of what we are going to be doing is bringing attention to inner phenomena that most of the modern world doesn't realize exist, and that are therefore difficult to bring into language because guess what? There are not words in English for much of this stuff.[1] In this way, much of what we are learning to attend to in autonomics is invisible both perceptually and linguistically to modern people. To use an analogy, this is sort of like feeling around for something in the dark of a cave. Your attention is the beam of light that you can direct into this darkness, and point at these aspects of your experience, so that you can begin to see them clearly.

As you can imagine, if you are not able to hold the beam steady, if it is shaking around, and jumping and twitching and darting off to check your instagram feed every few minutes, it is going to be a lot harder to find these things in the dark that you may be seeing for the first time with clarity in your life. If you are going to look deeply inward you need to be able to hold the light steady. So train in mindfulness. And, also, something very simple that all of us can do that helps to naturally re-enforce the stability of attention? Put down that fucking phone. Neurologically, it is like having a cocaine pacifier in our pockets. It is literally re-wiring us to be distracted all the time. You would not give your toddler a cocaine pacifier. Constrain your own.

---

1   This is why I wrote a book called Keywords: A Field Guide to the Missing Words, that addresses lexical gaps in the English language.

ATTENTION IS A FLASHLIGHT, AND AUTONOMIC SKILLS ARE GROUNDED IN HOW SKILLFULLY YOU CAN POINT AND STEADY IT

PRACTICE: BODY SCAN

Most traditions from around the world that work with awareness have some version of a body scan. The simplest version of this involves going someplace that you feel safe, allowing your eyes to close, and bringing attention inward to the sensations of the body. Our aim here is not to think about how the body feels, but to sense inwardly. Sometimes people scan the body moving from bottom to top. Sometimes people focus in on a particular area, such as the belly. Or the heart. Or the sensations of the breath.

If you attempt this and it either
1) doesn't feel good, or
2) the body doesn't feel available to sensation

Modify the practice in the following manner. First, allow the eyes to remain open. Then, starting with the breath, notice whether it feels best to
a) bring your attention inward to the sensations of the breath in the body
b) wrap your attention like a blanket around your body and feel the breath from there
c) feel your breath from outside your body

Allow your attention to sense your body from whichever location feels best to you. As you work through this book, don't ever close your eyes until it feels good to your body (never force them). And allow your sense of what feels good to govern how you use your attention. If it's useful you can use the body map on the facing page to map where you experienced sensation in the body. You could color in the places where it was easy to feel sensation, or the places where it was not. You could color code pleasant versus unpleasant sensations.

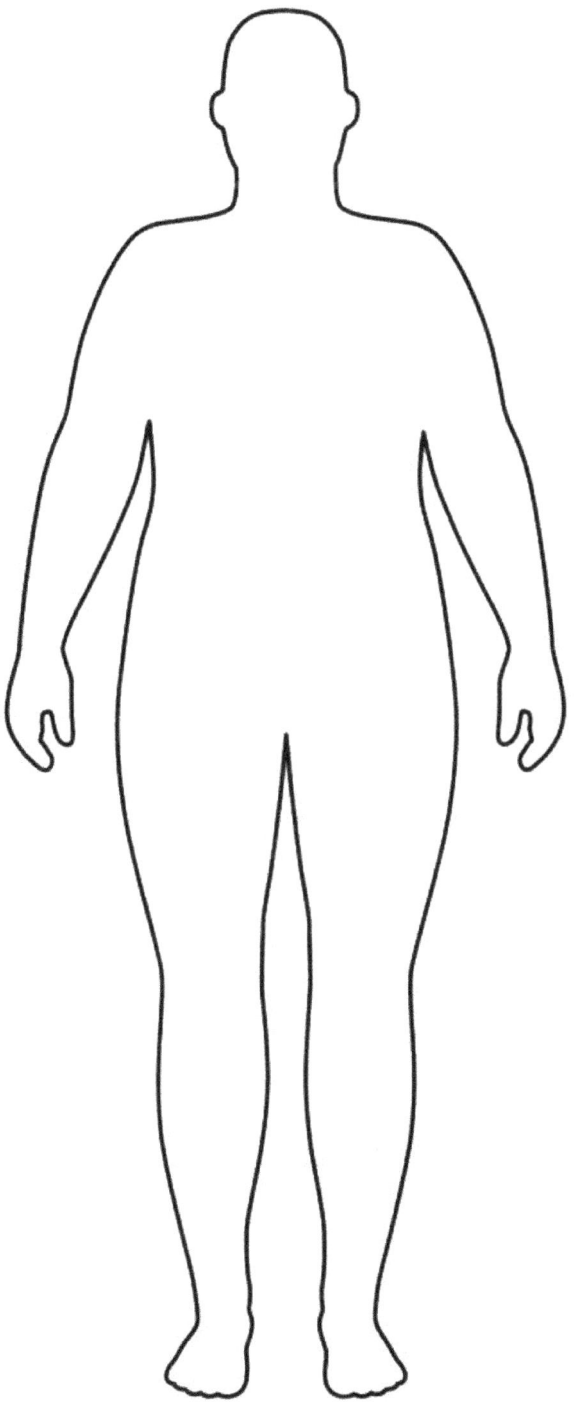

09- FIRST DIRECTIVE

Because the fundamental concern of your Autonomic Nervous System is your survival, its first calculation is always whether or not you feel safe, in danger, or under lifethreat. This calculation is happening all the time, literally with every breath. Each time we exhale, the fine-tuning of our ANS updates.

Most of the time we are not aware of this function– but if you are startled by something– let's say an object coiled up on the ground that you catch in your peripheral vision– it may have already responded by the time you consciously realize what it is reacting to. By the time your ordinary sense of self notices the black garden hose coiled on the ground, you've already jumped back, because a split-second before, your ANS, detecting this potential threat, already caused you to reflexively jump away.

This system is making use of billions of years of embodied evolutionary threat responses. Some part of your innate biology, with ancestral memory accumulated over hundreds of millions of years, knows that dark coils on the ground are usually snakes, and many of them are poisonous, and that if we don't get out of the way we might be dead.

This is amazing. Autonomic circuitry can respond without sending a signal all the way up to your cranial brain. When you jumped back, that circuit didn't take the ordinary voluntary movement pathway from your legs to your brainstem, to your midbrain dopaminergic motor pathways and back– it used an autonomic shortcut to save time.

In the wake of this response, your heart is probably pounding a bit. You might break out in a sweat. You might exclaim, and then get upset with yourself when you realize you freaked out over a hose. And this too is important, because it shows how much energy can be mobilized by the ANS in a split-second: how strongly it makes us respond physically *and* emotionally. The ANS mobilizes very large amounts of energy when it needs to. And the first job of your ANS is to keep you safe. That is directive numero uno.

So whenever we are assessing autonomic state, the first question we have to learn to ask ourselves is – *In the present moment, do I feel safe, in danger, or under lifethreat?*

Now, let's take a moment with this question. Because how do you know if you feel safe, in danger, or under lifethreat? Most people are not accustomed to asking themselves this question. And I'm not talking about *what you think*. What you think, in words and pictures, is not that important to this calculation. What is important is how your body *feels* about this.

So now I want you to ask me is– *Gabriel, what do you mean by that?*

Here's what I mean. In each and every present moment, you have a neural faculty that is assessing, in basically the same way that a thermometer assesses temperature, whether you are safe, in danger, or under lifethreat. If the status changes suddenly, we often know this by how our body reacts, as in this case where we jump back from the 'snake.' How our body reacts can tell us, after the fact, the degree of threat.

This temperature is also something that we can get used to, even if it is not ideal. Humans can get used to nearly anything, and if your autonomic temperature is too hot for long enough, or too cold, you just start thinking that *you* are too hot or too cold. There is a technical name for this moment-to-moment embodied neurological detection of safety, danger, or lifethreat, and it was coined by Stephen Porges, PhD, one of the world's leading experts on the relationship between the Autonomic Nervous System and behavior, and my principal mentor in neurophysiology.

This neural assessment is called *Neuroception.*

SNAILS ARE THE SIMPLEST WAY TO UNDERSTAND NEUROCEPTION.

10- SNAILS

Snails are the simplest way to understand neuroception.

A snail has an armored shell that it can withdraw inside of for protection. Once it pulls back into its shell, it is very safe from predators, but it cannot do anything. It cannot live.

It cannot feed, or explore, or pee, or poop, or have snail sex. They must, right? Otherwise, no more snails. Once it pulls back inside of this defensive perimeter, it is safe but it cannot live.

Once the danger is passed, it can potentially open up, and then extend itself out into the world. But the snail is soft-bodied, and so the more it extends itself, the more vulnerable it becomes. I'm not a snail, so I don't really know this, but I suppose it is the paradox of being a snail: the more you live out loud, the more vulnerable you are. The more you hunker down for safety, the less you live.

Neuroception is the opening of the snail shell. It is the thermometer at the mouth of the snail shell deciding whether or not we'll open up into safety and connection (availability) or pull back into danger and lifethreat (defense).

We need to be able to do both. Sometimes we are safe, and sometimes we are not. If we couldn't pull back into defense, we couldn't endure dangerous and lifethreating situations. But if we get stuck in the biology of defense, we cannot flourish.

The question for modern people is the following: based on how many times we have gotten hurt, are we willing to continue to learn how to extend out of the shell when there is enough safety? Most modern people do not, and therefore most modern people are not well. Remaining in defense is fundamentally incompatible with flourishing.

11- SELF AS WATER

Let's say you'd never been to earth. I know, I know. You're like
- *Gabriel, I'm here right now.* But let's just say. And let's just say
that I am your guide, and that the first element of the earth
situation that I'm going to introduce you to is water.

I might explain that one of the unique features of this terres-
trial globe, this stunning blue and green marble spinning in the
vastness of celestial space is this element that we have here, an
everyday mystery: water.

Water is the very story of Life. That it comprises seventy
percent of your bodily mass and cycles through you in mineral-
rich inward rivers, streams, and tributaries you know as the
blood pulsing through your circulatory system. And so without
further fanfare, into your hands I place a cup of water. And I
invite you to drink, and so you do.

You feel the liquid flowing down your throat, and this particular water, from a glacial spring, is flinty and cold and tastes like
life herself, although there is no word for this in your language.
And I ask you to touch water, and so you pour some across
your fingers, and she is cold and wet, and you observe her crystalline clarity in the glint of the alpine sun.

Water, we intone together.

And then, let us say, just for fun, I whisk you away, and we find
ourselves moving at speed into the atmosphere, up to about
thirty thousand feet, where we suddenly stop in the middle of
a Cumulonimbus cloud. Vapor is everywhere. We are blinded
and hemmed in by whiteness. And I say I would like to introduce you to water, wearing another of her faces. And to me you
might say, "I just met water, and this is not water."

But of course it is. That is the thing about this mysterious

element, this substance that lives on the threshold between spirit and matter: a deep mystery in her own right. Water that transforms its molecular structure in response to the *kotodama* (a Japanese word for the spiritual interior of the word) of the words we speak to her. Just ask Masuro Emoto, the eminent Japanese researcher of water, who has filmed her crystalline structure modifying in realtime based on the energetic signature of the words spoken to her. Speak to water with love, she hums into crystalline harmonics. Speak to her with loathing, and she denatures into unwieldy blobs. Mysterious indeed.

We are mostly water. You probably know this already. And I have just introduced you to two of the faces water wears, but there is a third: ice.

Water can exist as liquid, as vapor (a gas), or as ice (a solid.) And our biosphere, unique among known worlds, provides her the conditions to transition between all three. She snows onto mountains as a solid, melts into rivers that merge with the ocean as liquid, evaporates back into the atmosphere as vapor.

So now to the neuroscience. What I would like to propose to you here is that you are elementally like water. This should come as no great surprise since 70% of what you are made of is her. But what may be new information is that your Autonomic Nervous System can, like water, exist in three states. There is a version of you that exists when you feel safe: the liquid water version. There is a version of you that exists when you feel in danger: the steam version. There is a version of you that exists when you feel under lifethreat: the ice version. And these might as well be three different people.

Like water wearing her three faces, you, wearing these three states, will be un-recognizable as the others. The liquid water version of you will bear as much resemblance to the steam version as steam does to liquid. The ice version of yourself as much resemblance to the steam version as ice to steam.

So, to flesh out our analogy– like water, the ANS can surface three distinct neural platforms, depending on whether we feel safe, in danger, or under lifethreat. Each of these foundations has distinct and discrete characteristics, leads to a particular worldview, and shapes both how it feels inside us and how we interpret what is around us. And our self as water does not recognize our self as steam or as ice. When we become steam we don't remember liquid water. As ice we don't remember steam. Do you understand? Because of how deep the ANS is in your neural architecture, most of the time you just inhabit the state. In steam, you wear steam-colored glasses. In ice, ice-colored glasses. And these are glasses you cannot take off.

Each state is entered by crossing a discrete threshold. Like water shifting from 99.9 degrees Celsius to 100 degrees, the process of moving across the threshold happens on a continuum. Sometimes it is slow-creeping, sometimes it moves almost instantaneously.

Yet from the perspective of the identity of water, once we shift across one of these states, we are different. We can become unrecognizable to another version of ourselves. Water, as ice, *IS* ice. It doesn't retain its identity as liquid. It doesn't remember what it felt like to be liquid. For us this can be a bit more complex because a person rarely becomes simply ice. But the parts of ourselves that are ice are locked out of the experience of being liquid water. If enough of us gets locked out of ourselves, gets stuck in the ice state, or the steam state– if our center of gravity stays here long enough or gets stuck here deep enough, we can forget that our original nature is liquid water. We get untethered from who we really are– dissociated from our original identity. Most people who are deeply seriously ill are humans who have turned, autonomically, to ice. Frighteningly, a fair number of them are running the world. We might note, as did indigenous elder Angaangaq Angakkorsuaq, that the polar icecaps will not stop melting until we can melt the ice in the heart of man.

YOU HAVE TO UNDERSTAND
WHAT STATE YOU ARE IN
TO KNOW WHAT KIND OF
EFFORT IS REQUIRED TO
BRING YOURSELF BACK TO
LIQUID WATER.

12- WARM IT OR COOL IT?

In the analogy of liquid water, the place that flourishing resides, is the liquid water version of yourself. But notice that we can get deviated from this by stress. Stress, which is threat, tends to move us out of the liquid water version of ourselves. It can move us into steam (fight-or flight), or if that is not far enough, it can move us into ice (shutdown, collapse). Autonomic fluency is important because you can cool ice all day long and nothing happens. And you can warm steam all day long and nothing happens. Understanding that you have two distinct foundational threat responses: one for danger, and one for lifethreat is practically very important. Because you have to understand what state you are in to know what kind of effort to apply to it to bring yourself back to liquid water. If we are in an ice state, we have to thaw it. And we have to understand the characteristics of ice. If we are going to thaw it, we have to warm it like the sun warms a living branch encased in ice by an icestorm. We have to apply effort in a particular way with an understanding of the needs of this state. Certain interventions will predictably help us move through this state, and others will not. If we are in a steam state, we have to condense it. We have to drop the temperature. And we need to understand practically how to do this. Certain interventions will predictably help us move through this state, and others will not. Finally, and this is a major thrust of our work, we want to learn how to deepen and expand the amount of liquid water in our system generally. Any part of you that is in steam or ice is, by definition, part of your awareness that has not succeeded in shifting back to liquid water. Let's notice here also– your nervous system is designed to allow you to shift into steam and ice. This is necessary for your survival. There is nothing wrong with steam or ice. They are both amazing! We need to be able to become both of these. The challenges arise for us when we get stuck in steam or ice and cannot get back to liquid water, start believing that we are steam or ice, forget that liquid water exists, or forget that we can find our way home to liquid water.

PRACTICE: SELF PORTRAIT AS WATER DROPLET

Visualize yourself as a droplet of water. Through the lens of the three states of water, take a moment to simply visualize yourself as a water droplet. Some part of this droplet is liquid water, some part of it steam, some part of it ice. Don't think too much about this. Let your imagining be instinctual. What we are aiming to do here, through autonomic fluency, is understand how to thaw ice and condense steam back to liquid water. We want to grow the *you* that is liquid water. In the space below, draw yourself as a water droplet. Allow the drawing to be both instinctual, intuitive, and also precise. Draw liquid water, steam, and ice if these states exist in your self portrait.

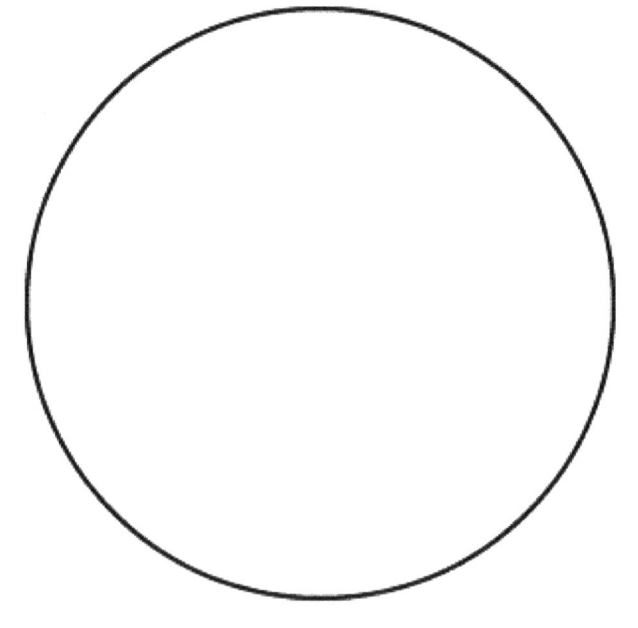

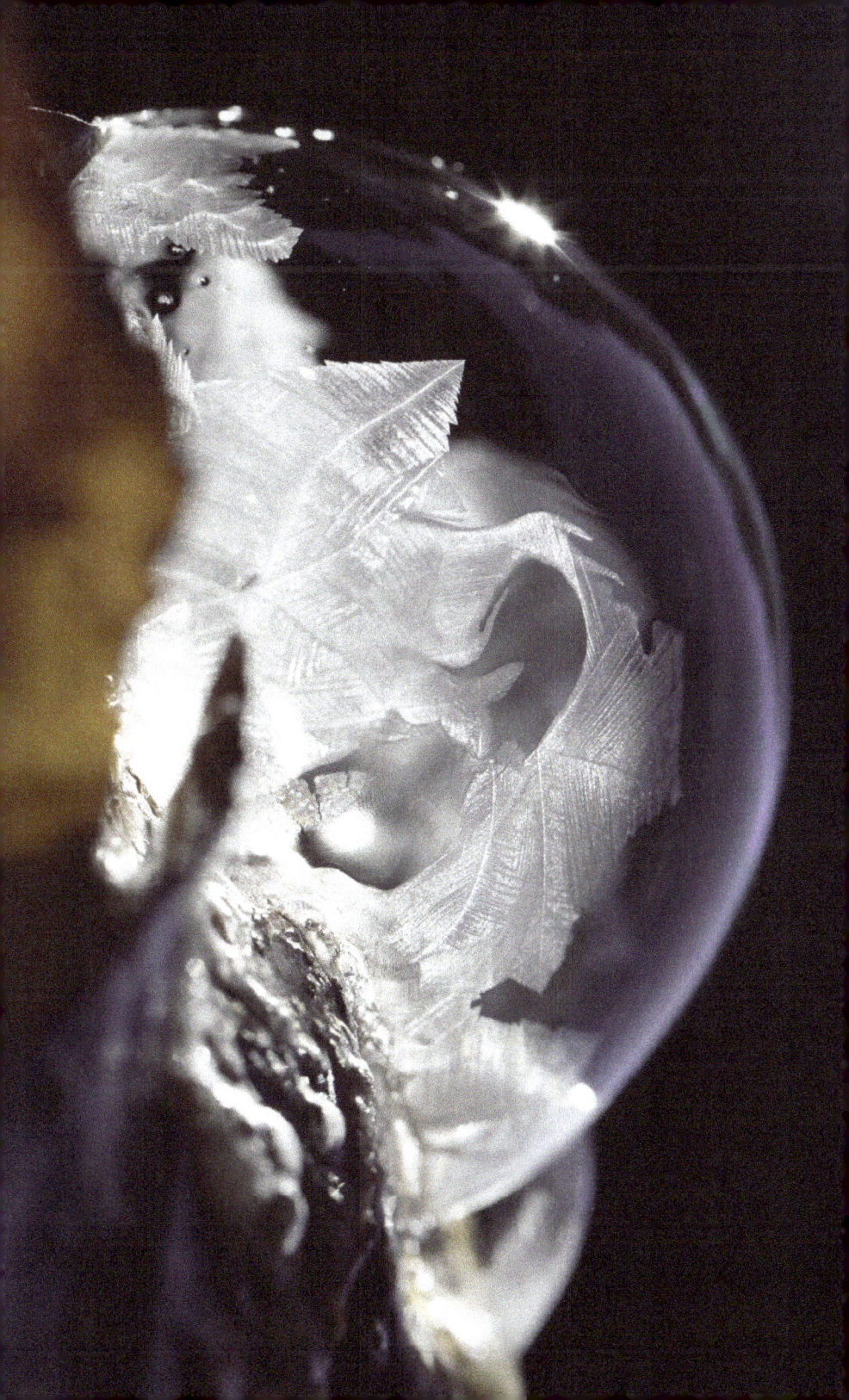

13- STATE IDENTIFICATION

There is an interesting question that arises here right away, as we begin to make the leap from an intuitive understanding of ice, steam, and water to a neurological one.

While most people, in their 'water droplet of self', have at least some steam and some ice, what is the neurological definition of being in one of those states of water? At a practical level, how are we to know where we are on the map?

So you don't get upset with me later, and feel like I've done a bait and switch on you, I'm going to teach you the three primary states now, but I want you to understand that the map of the Autonomic Nervous System that we call the autonomic mandala has twelve states on it. They are all derived from this fundamental question about safety, danger, and lifethreat, but they express twelve of the most common autonomic states that we have seen over the past decade working with tens of thousands of people from fifty countries around the world.

In our simplified triangular map at left, safety is the top left, danger is the top right, and lifethreat is straight down. These locations correspond to liquid water (upper left), steam (upper right), and ice (down). Let's walk through how each of these locations feels at a visceral level in the body.

We are bringing attention here to something that you have been experiencing since you were tiny, but that most people are not aware of as a pattern language. And so as you start to bring attention to this, I want to ask you to be gentle with yourself, and also to begin to think about your experience through the lens of these foundational states.

It's a bit like tuning into a radio station on an old-fashioned stereo, where you may have to adjust the dial finely with your fingers to tune into the station where these clear signals are coming from. Don't be upset with yourself if you cannot feel this right away. Just sort of point your listening in this direction, and see if you can begin to sense it: if any part of the description resonates with you.

LIQUID WATER

The liquid water version of yourself will feel like your best self. When you think back on periods of life when you felt like you were flourishing, these are likely liquid water periods. When you are in the liquid water state you will
- feel like yourself
- experience a sense of homecoming
- feel a sense of ease or 'naturalness'
- the body will feel appropriately tensioned
- this means feeling relaxed when resting, feeling intense when exerting
- breathing will be able to deepen naturally
- you will feel your feet on the ground
- you will move easily
- you will have access to strategic thinking
- you will be able to plan

- you will be able to do what you say you are going to do
- thinking will be clear
- the unfamiliar may seem exciting and adventurous

STEAM

The steam version of yourself can come in one of two flavors. This is because it is a fight *or* flight response. Fight and flight are actually quite different in feeling tone, but they are both high-energy states, and they are both mobilized, which means that the body wants to move. So both fight-and-flight states share the following characteristics

- your body will feel on edge and alert
- your body will want to move
- your heart rate will be elevated, even standing still
- your eyes will be searching for something
- it will be hard for you to catch your breath or breathe deeply
- being still will not feel good
- your natural inclination will be to *do something*
- your muscles will feel tense
- if you are a teeth grinder, this will happen
- your head will tilt forward on your neck, so the junction at the base of the skull will be tense and sore
- you will be very aware of who is with you and who is against you, creating a physiological sense of 'us' versus 'them'
- the unfamiliar will seem dangerous

Beyond these general body tunings, the energy and emotional tone of steam depends on whether you are moving into a flight response or a fight response. If you are moving into flight you will experience

- a sense that something is wrong
- an awareness of everything that could go wrong
- a feeling of nervousness, jumpiness, fearfulness, or

anxiety
- energy moving into your feet and legs, restless legs
- you may want to run
- if you ignore this or suppress this, you may find yourself becoming more anxious
- you will perceive the world around you as dangerous
- you will be seeking to get away from something
- what you are seeking to get away from could be something in your external environment, or something in your internal environment

If you get stuck in this state, you will have difficulty recalibrating. Suddenly, the world will just seem dangerous, and you will just feel like you cannot get safe. What is unfamiliar will feel frightening.

This is different from moving into fight, where you will

- find blood flowing into your arms and hands
- start to wonder how come everyone is so stupid
- discover that lots of things are pissing you off
- find yourself feeling increasingly confrontational
- be drawn to increasingly aggressive music
- want to move toward whatever you are upset with
- want to pick a fight with someone or something[1]

If you get stuck in this state, you will have difficulty recalibrating. Suddenly, the world will just seem filled with idiots, and everyone and everything will be pissing you off all the time. The unfamiliar will seem irritating.

ICE

When we transition across the threshold from steam to ice, and move into shutdown, this is characterized by

---

1 If we are deeply in the grip of this state, it can seem like rocks are glaring at us.

- feelings of surreality or events being dreamlike
- spaciness, numbness, feeling withdrawn
- feeling slow or woozy
- the body feeling lethargic, or drugged, or underwater
- feeling stuck
- the spine collapsing, the chest falling in, the belly collapsing
- no muscle tone in the deep belly
- being unable to think clearly
- feeling extremely overwhelmed
- decision-making paralysis
- immobilization
- losing contact with your ordinary sense of self
- losing contact with the ground (it may feel like you are floating)
- losing contact with the body, to which you may not feel tethered
- in an ice state, there is neural inhibition on breath, which means that it will feel forced

If you get stuck in this state, you will have difficulty recalibrating. Suddenly, you will be stuck. Your life will be on hold. You will not be able to move forward. Everything will feel unfamiliar and disorienting.

As you can probably sense from this list, there is a fundamental correlation between being stuck in a not-liquid state and various mental and physical health issues. Pretty much any time that you find yourself in a chronic or enduring steam or ice state, it will have negative health repercussions. These will always include both physical (body) and mental (psychological) symptoms, although for most people one side or the other of this will be more acute, or more distressing, so that will generally be the thing that they seek treatment for, or help managing.

You can probably see pretty clearly that getting stuck in an ice state (a shutdown response) correlates really closely with withdrawal, anti-social behavior, clinical depression. You can probably see pretty clearly that getting stuck in a flight response leads to experiencing anxiety, which, if it endures, can quickly become clinical-grade. You can probably see pretty clearly how getting stuck in a fight response leads to feeling angry ALL THE TIME.

It is really important to notice that our response to a threat is a function of how our nervous system perceives it, so that what makes one person anxious may make another person angry. This is reductionist for sure, but financial insecurity might make your mom worried and your dad pissed off. People are less likely (maybe I should say *men* are less likely) to seek clinical support for feeling angry than women are for feeling anxious. Rather, men are more likely to begin self-medicating.

If I cannot get my body to shut down its arousal response, which basically feels like the volume is turned up too high on aggression, and I know this, I will seek out things that blunt that experience. I might begin drinking alcohol, which, as a CNS depressant, is a costly but effective solution. It is costly because I am likely to become addicted. It is effective because it downshifts this steam state, making the internal milieu tolerable. If I'm stuck in a flight state, I might take up smoking cigarettes. Again, a costly but effective solution, because nicotine has very strong anti-anxiety properties.

One of the most important things to recognize here is that the way people self-medicate is never random. It tells us an extraordinary amount about what is out of balance autonomically. The precise way in which people self medicate is our deepest clue to what ails them, because it is their solution to a deeper problem that we cannot see.

I once worked with a twelve-year old boy who was incarcerated, and had been addicted to crystal meth. He was using so heavily that he had suffered a heart attack. Given the price he had paid for using the drug, given that continued use was likely to make his teeth fall out, and given that I was working with him in Juvenile Hall, it took me a long time to wrap my head around why he was doing this to himself. But that was because I didn't understand the chemistry. Crystal meth is extraordinarily effective at alleviating depression. Methamphetamines were, in fact, the very first anti-depressant prescribed in the United States.

The young man I was working with had a serious trauma history, a terrible home life, and a totally unstable living situation. This was debilitatingly depressing. And so, since he didn't have access to compassionate and skilled counseling or psychiatric care, he had turned to the street pharmacy. And the drug he chose was a costly and effective solution.

If the psychological state you find yourself in is unendurable, most of us will choose a costly yet effective solution over no solution at all. Many of the pharmaceuticals on the street have an analog in conventional medicine. As anyone who has ever been in unendurable pain knows, opioids are absolutely fucking amazing. That is why your body endogenously manufactures fifty different types of them. It is why when doctors prescribe them people have a hard time putting them down and physicians have a hard time not writing the scripts. It is why people get addicted to heroine, which is called, in conventional medicine, morphine. Same pharmacological effects: different dispensing protocol. The street version has social stigma attached to it, the medical version does not.

Most of us are spending a lot more time self-medicating than we realize. I want you to recognize that there a range of self-medicating responses that most of us engage in daily to adjust the parameters on our Autonomic Nervous Systems without ever realizing this is what we are doing.

Let's be really clear that we are not judging this behavior. We are just noticing it. You can be self-medicating when

- you eat sugar
- you drink coffee
- potato chips, yum
- comfort food
- chocolate, fuck yes
- you reach for your phone
- social media
- gaming
- you smoke a cigarette
- you drink alcohol
- you have sex
- pornography
- you exercise
- you meditate

The point I am making here is not that these things are bad necessarily. Meditation bad? The point I am making is that most of us do them reflexively, by which I mean without conscious awareness, because we know (our bodies know) that they will alter our autonomic inputs in some predictable way. My point is that all of the above are interventions with neurological and chemical effects, and what matters is how and why we use them. I know people who meditate because they cannot metabolize their own emotions. This is not what meditation is supposed to be for.

There are times when I've started craving chocolate suddenly, and then realized I was stressed out. Which is to say that just like jumping back from the snake, the Autonomic Nervous System has already solved the problem (*Whoa! Who put this delicious piece of chocolate in my mouth to resolve a problem my conscious mind didn't realize I had? Oh look, it was me!*)

Part of the autonomic fluency that we are developing is to begin to notice our autonomic solutions to deeper problems that we are not aware of, and then to be able to more intentionally choose our response.

Often, a more intentional response simply involves noticing first. I cannot address the problem until I am aware that it has arisen. If I can catch myself before I've eaten the entire chocolate bar, I can go - *What just happened? Why am I feeling stressed out? What just put me into a flight response?* Understanding that gives me more leverage and more options in terms of how I choose to respond. I can shift from reacting to making a conscious choice, which is always better, because reactions tend to have unintended consequences, whereas choices are deliberate.

THE WAY PEOPLE SELF-MEDICATE IS NOT RANDOM. PART OF THE AUTONOMIC FLUENCY THAT WE ARE DEVELOPING IS TO NOTICE OUR AUTONOMIC SOLUTIONS TO DEEPER PROBLEMS THAT WE ARE NOT AWARE OF, AND THEN TO BE ABLE TO MORE INTENTIONALLY CHOOSE OUR RESPONSE.

HOW ARE YOU SELF-MEDICATING?

14- NEUROLOGY

Earlier in the book, before I had really defined these terms, I said that autonomic state was comprised of three variables: neuroception (the snail), neurology, and neurochemistry.

When we talk about autonomic physiology as a field, what most people are talking about is the second component of this: the underlying neurology.

My mentor Stephen W. Porges is famous for developing the Polyvagal Theory, which is the first model of autonomic physiology that identified multiple vagal systems. The theory is called poly- (Latin for *many*) vagal, which is a reference to the Vagus nerve, the 10th cranial nerve, and its differentiation into multiple systems.

The vagus is the primary (though not the only) neural conduit of the Autonomic Nervous System. Before it was called the vagus is was known as the pneumo-gastric nerve (as in lungs & guts). *Vagus* means wanderer in Latin, and like a meandering river, the vagal systems wind through the body, innervating organs throughout the viscera, and winding up to the brain.

You will notice that I'm saying winding up to the brain, rather than winding down from the brain, and the reason that I'm saying this is because most of the neural fibers in the vagus are conveying sensory information from the interior of the body inward and upward.

The vagus is an inward listening system. It is, in actuality, the largest sensory organ that you have, and its listening is pointed inward. Its job is to monitor and modulate the functioning of all of your interior bodily systems, based on information from within and outside the body.

As I said in the **FIRST DIRECTIVE** chapter, survival is the first im-

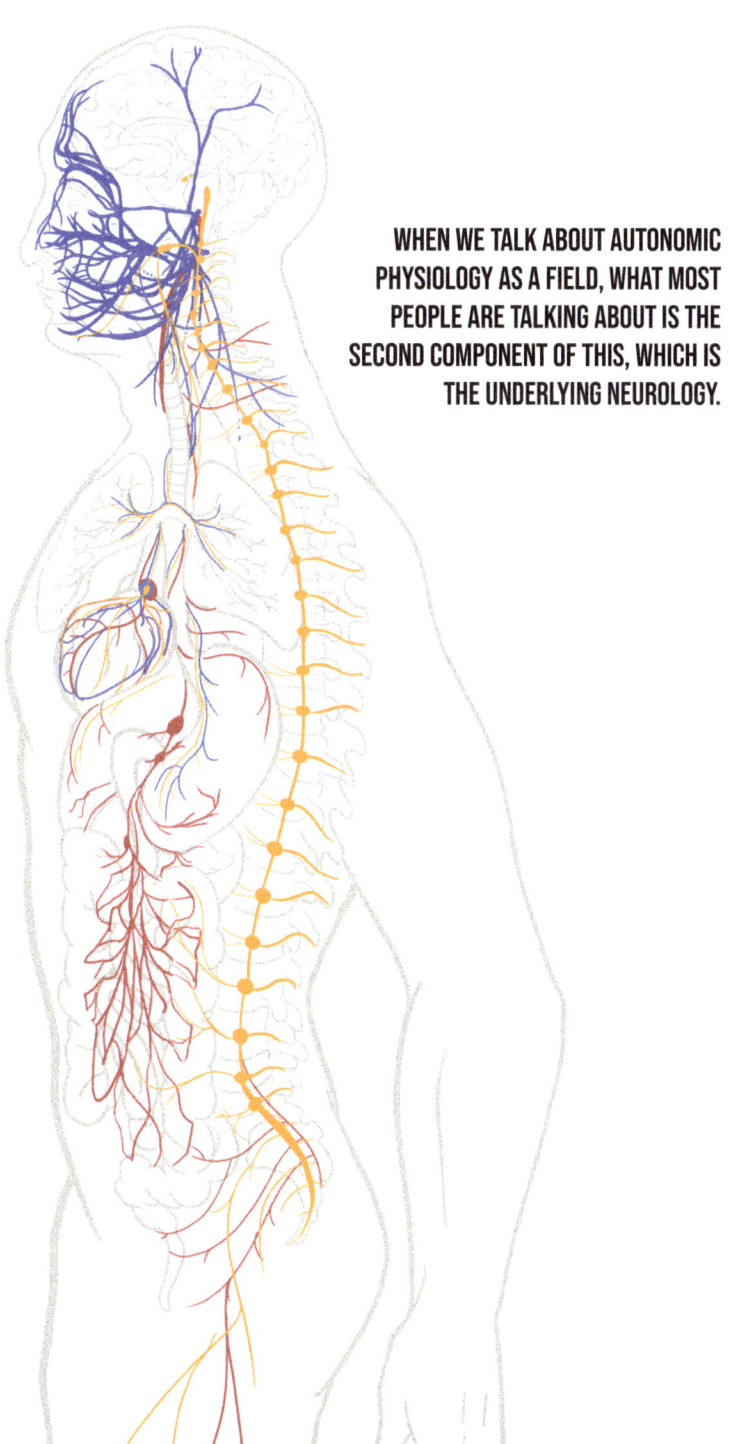

WHEN WE TALK ABOUT AUTONOMIC PHYSIOLOGY AS A FIELD, WHAT MOST PEOPLE ARE TALKING ABOUT IS THE SECOND COMPONENT OF THIS, WHICH IS THE UNDERLYING NEUROLOGY.

perative of the body, and so neurology and the way it is tuned is derivative of our neuroceptive (snail) sensing of safety, danger, and lifethreat.

Neuroception creates the context in the which the Autonomic Nervous System activates or inhibits three primary neurological systems.

Porges was the first person to recognize that what we call the vagus is not simply a nerve: it is a conduit. In the same way that when they dig up your street to put in a pipe, they will bundle together telephone lines, cable, and other utilities, the vagus is a conduit that holds multiple functional neural systems that are distinct.

The way that Stephen Porges discerned this is one of the great detective stories of 20th century neuroscience, because he basically reverse-engineered the understanding from studying paradoxical readings in infant heart rate variability. Based on seeing two opposing actions of the vagus, he deduced that a single nerve could not be responsible for both contradictory effects on the heart.

Porges' breakthrough, in the form of understanding these two vagal systems, one of which is really ancient, unmyelinated, and localized primarily in the guts, and the other that is much newer evolutionarily, and integrates the heart, face, and hands profoundly transformed our understanding of how the ANS functions.

Yet Porges' model falls short of functional mapping because it was built on faulty anatomical maps that Porges inherited, fails to differentiate neurology from chemistry, and fails to understand how the autonomic systems relate across the continuum of experience.

You have three autonomic systems. They are localized in different areas of the body, serve different needs, and coordinate differing behavioral responses.

There are three autonomic systems in the human body:

in BLUE, a **Connection System** comprised of the ventral branch of the vagus that unites the neural regulation of the face, voice, eyes, ears, and turning of the head and neck, with the heart and breath in newborns. As this system myelinates it grows into the ventral surfaces of the hands, parts of the ventral surface of the feet, the skin and the genitals. When this system is driving, we experience health-creating states.

in YELLOW, a **Movement System** organized along the entire length of the spine and into the brainstem whose central pattern generators govern rhythmic movements in the body including sucking/swallowing, breathing, the movements of the arms and legs, the movements required to pee, poop, and experience an orgasm. This system has been understood by classical neurology and Polyvagal Theory primarily with respect to undergirding the fight-flight responses (it is known in classical neurology as the Sympathetic Nervous System), yet this is only how it operates when threat is detected and activation chemistry is present. It coordinates all centrally pattern generated movement (crawling, walking, running, swimming, complex coordinated arm swings, coordinated full spinal movement patterns, sucking, swallowing, vomiting, breathing, digesting, peeing, pooping, sexual thrusting/ hip rotational range, orgasm, etc). When we refer to danger responses from this system we will use the terminology 'fight/flight response'. In this configuration, it is part of our response repertoire to neuroceptions of danger.

in RED, a **Grounding System** comprised of the dorsal branch of the vagus that innervates the deep belly primarily beneath the respiratory diaphragm and includes the enteric nervous system. This system has been understood by Polyvagal Theory and the related somatically-oriented trauma healing modalities only in the configuration that it enters when we experience lifethreat, and is referred to by Polyvagal Theory as the Dorsal Vagal System. Yet it is actually the *hara* (Japanese), or *lower dantien* (Chinese), understood in eastern cultures to be the 'elixir field': the location where the elixir of life is made. This grounding system is the center of metabolism, the center of authentic movement. When we are referring to the role of this system in lifethreat responses, we will call it the 'Shutdown System'.

The presence of safety, which creates rhythms in the body, co-ordinates the activities of the Connection System, Movement System, and Grounding System so that when you feel safe enough, you are able to draw on the intelligence of all three systems. These states are health-creating.

These are the **LIQUID WATER** states.

When you move into detection of danger, this rhythmic-ity withdraws, you lose the coordination of the Connection System, the direction of information flow reverses from being centered in the guts and heart to being centered in the brain, and activation chemistry is released by the HPA Axis (hypo-thalamic-pituitary-adrenal), giving rise to the continuum of fight-or-flight states.

These are the **STEAM** states.

When you move into detection of lifethreat, shutdown chem-istry of endogenous opioids is released, movement withdraws, the body immobilizes, and you move into the continuum of shutdown states.

These are the **ICE** states.

YOUR NEUROCHEMISTRY
IS AN INWARD OCEAN

15- CHEMISTRY

While it makes sense to think of your nervous system as an electrical system, with electrical pulses being fired rapidly down the fibers of nerves, your neurochemistry is part of an inward ocean.

As nerves develop in your body, they always are twinned with blood supply. So it makes sense to think of your nervous system as part of a larger neuro-vascular system. This system puts your neurology into contact with another manner in which it can be influenced from within the body: hormonally.

Hormonal communication in the body is different than neural communication. It works through the medium of the blood, and in the same way that when you add a drop of ink to water, you can watch it slowly spread out and percolate, the circulation of hormones through our system is a diffusion process.

The fact that we can shift into a fight-or-flight response, activated by the neuroception of danger, and the sudden release of adrenaline, shows us that hormones can act quickly. In light of the necessity to diffuse this chemical messenger throughout the body, elevated heart rate, which essentially stirs the inward ocean more quickly, makes a lot of sense.

What I'm referring to here as neurochemistry are classes of hormones that engage in specific ways with our neurology. The scope of this interaction is in fact, extraordinarily refined. Our bodies manufacture an incredible number of hormones. They control everything from regulating our circadian rhythms, to metabolism, to the female ovulatory and male ejaculatory cycles. Yet I'm going to restrict our conversation about hormones here to a discussion of three primary chemistries that directly influence the ANS.

These are the connection chemistry of love and pair-bonding.

The neurochemistry of activation. And the neurochemistry of shutdown. As you are learning about these chemistries, I'd like to invite you to see if you can feel their signatures. The names of the chemicals are less important than a felt sense of their properties. How does it feel when you are under their influence? Like a sort of intoxicating chemical musk, each of these hormones can rapidly change the inner weather of your mood, the way the body feels, and how it works.

Connection chemistry requires us to feel safe in order to release. The most famous connection hormone is oxytocin, which is released during orgasm, nursing, experiences of love, and pair-bonding. The sort of glow you experience during, and in the wake of an orgasm is produced by oxytocin. If you think about how long this feeling endures, you also have some sense of the half-life of this neuropeptide, which is about three to six minutes. Oxytocin is the chemistry of intimacy, of Union. [1]

It has a profoundly different felt quality than adrenaline and cortisol, the signatures of activation. When we are startled by something, or move into a threat response, the body releases adrenaline and cortisol. If you want to get a glimpse of adrenaline and cortisol release in the absence of a threat response, think about early Robin Williams or Richard Pryor delivering a standup routine. The manic energy, the constant frantic nonstop talk? What you are witnessing is the energy of cocaine, but what cocaine does, in the body, in addition to altering dopamine and serotinon levels, is release massive amounts of adrenaline. Its release of dopamine and serotonin are important, because these create euphoria. In their absence, with just the adrenaline, you get massively sped-up, frantic, high intensity activation. [2] While the half-life of adrenaline is 2-3 min-

---

1 For purposes of simplicity in this text I am not going to address the role of vasopressin, with which oxytocin works in partnership. If you want to go deeper into this chemistry, and these neurologies, I direct you to *The Neurobiology of Connection.*

2   I am not celebrating cocaine use, but if you'd like to view the same person doing standup while on cocaine, versus not, so that you can discern the energetic signature of the drug, watch *John*

utes in blood plasma, its release in a fight-or-flight response takes up to 20 minutes to clear. This is why, once it gets going, a fight-or-flight response tails off slowly. It explains why, once a person gets really upset, it takes a while to calm back down– you are still high on endogenous chemistry of activation.

The third autonomically-relevant chemistry for us to consider are the endogenous opioids released under lifethreat. The body will release a cascade of enkephalins in response to lifethreat events. Evolutionarily, lifethreat responses are linked with a bodily anticipation of impending death. If you are going to be eaten by a tiger, you don't want to feel it. The release of endogenous opioids are connected to immobilization and dissociation. Their signature energy is the experience of being in an altered state– a dreamlike or surreal quality. When, in the wake of a traumatic event, people talk about having been 'outside of their bodies' or 'watching [my]self from above', these experiences of dissociation are gated by endogenous opioids. Endogenous opioids, which are designed to kill pain, have the longest half-life of any autonomically-involved neurochemistry. Unlike the others, there are times where, in the wake of a traumatic exposure, they do not clear from the system at all.

Mulaney: *Kid Gorgeous at Radio City* from 2018 (cocaine), then watch *John Mulaney: Baby J* from 2023 (post-cocaine). I'm not talking about what he says, I'm talking about the felt quality of the delivery. The difference is staggering. Neurochemically, cocaine is a form of liquid swagger. The allure becomes apparent: another very high-cost form of self-medicating.

16- AUTONOMIC SPECTRUM

Now that we have considered the three components that combine to produce an autonomic state, lets settle into the final analogy that we will use to build our model.

Every kindergartner learns that yellow and blue makes green, red and yellow makes orange, and blue and red make purple. In the model below, around the primary triangle (safety, danger, lifethreat) we have introduced a color wheel. This gives you a sense of twelve combinations and their various relationships to the primary geography of neuroception. Each of these colors represents an autonomic state.

Those states from 8 o'clock to 12 o'clock are largely health-creating. States from 1 o'clock to 4 o'clock are danger responses, and states from 5 o'clock to 7 o'clock are lifethreat responses.

17- THE AUTONOMIC COMPASS

You know what a compass is: an instrument that helps you find your way home if you are lost. A compass doesn't have to be a metal disc, though that's what most of us think of. A small metal disk with a magnetic needle balanced delicately on a pivot. You hold it in the palm of your hand, flat, so that the needle can float, and the needle wobbles until it finds North.

A compass could simply be knowing which side of the trees more lichen grows on. Or which direction the prevailing winds tend to blow. Or the direction of a prominent visible landmark like a mountain. Or that if you travel down to the bottom of the valley there will be a watercourse, and if you follow that long enough it will lead to a larger watercourse, which will eventually lead to the Bay. By which I mean that you can internalize the compass; it doesn't have to be something *out there*. A compass is a tool that helps you orient to an environment, even if you've never been there before, and determine the coordinates you need to follow to get to where you need to go. It is a tool of orientation, a tool of navigation, of cartography. A tool you can turn to if you are lost; a tool that will help you get home.

Your Autonomic Nervous System contains the most powerful biological levers that govern your thriving. Its function governs the deepest root drivers of our wellbeing. It is the biological system with the most control of any over your direct moment-to-moment experience of wellbeing. And yet most modern people don't even know what it is.

The Autonomic Compass on the following pages is a tool that you can use to help you decipher the readings that your Autonomic Nervous System is giving you. A compass that can help you figure out– *Huh, what is the information that my Autonomic Nervous System is giving me, and how can I translate that into guidance that will get me home?* Because make no mistake, your

Autonomic Nervous System is giving you guidance all of the time, because that it what it does. You know what that guidance is?

The way that you feel.

Your inner weather. Whether it is sunny or stormy, calm or agitated. Your moment-to-moment experience of how it feels to be you, the you-in-your-body, the you-in-your-mind, all of this is your autonomic landscape. The readings are present in your voice, your face, your gesture, your posture, your emotional tone, your heartrate, your breathing. How open and available or closed and defended you feel. Whether you have access to flow states or feel shut down. All of this is autonomic terrain.

Most people are just stuck in their current autonomic weather, because it is where they find themselves. If the weather endures for long enough, people identify with their weather. They are like, *Oh, yeah, I live in Portland: it rains a lot. This weather– it is who I am.*

People just get accustomed to the weather that is happening. If you spend enough time feeling in danger, and this manifests as a flight response, and because you don't know how ground into this it turns into anxiety, and that endures, you start to think you are an anxious person.

You begin attributing permanent characterological traits to what is essentially an adaptive defensive response. Your body's solution to feeling under threat. The moment you begin assigning permanence to this response it is no longer adaptive. You have decided it is your baseline: part of your identity.

But another way to approach this is to figure out why you are spending your life feeling in danger, and work to transform that. Medicine treats the defensive responses of the Autonomic Nervous System as symptoms that need to be fixed. Autonomics treats responses of the Autonomic Nervous System as your body's compass: it's best present solution to a deeper problem that we cannot see. If anxiety is the solution your body has found, we have to ask the question— *What is it a solution to?*

And the answer to this is *threat.* If we are willing to consider that the body's solution is meaningful— that feeling anxious is not random, arbitrary, a misguided response, or a malfunction, that it is giving us compass directions, so to speak, we can use it as information to address the thing that is causing it, which is the underlying threat it is a response to.

Wellness Provider and client:

Did you feel anxious yesterday?

No.

Do you feel anxious today?

Yes.

If we assume that is an intelligent response of the body, did something happen that might be making you feel that way?

Put in a slightly different way, when it comes to stress responses, the western medical approach is to smash the compass. *Oh, you are feeling anxious. Let's turn that compass off because it is giving us an uncomfortable reading!* We medicate the symptoms, essentially telling the body— stop giving us these uncomfortable directional signals! Yet if you break the compass, you make it much harder for it to do its job, which is to give you reliable readings about what you need to do to get home. [1]

---

1 This sounds like I am making a blanket condemnation of pharmaceutical intervention, which I am not. What I am pointing your attention to is the worldview from which it derives. Sometimes pharmacology is necessary. But the worldview from which most prescriptions are written is problematic because discomfort and pain have meaning. Sometimes it is beyond our adaptational capacity to endure, but even then it is a meaningful signal. If we instead regard

A great deal of what we have been taught is *psychological* (it's all in your head!) is actually *physiological* (it is in your body). In plain language, things that you have been taught are abstract, familial, based on relationships with your parents from early childhood, their relationships with their parents, your familial lineage, do originate in that. But if you boil them down to their essence, the thing at the heart of them is the embodied adaptations your Autonomic Nervous System has made to feeling unsafe. And no amount of insight or compassion will transform this. Talk therapy has no bearing on it whatsoever. Because it has nothing to do with what you think at all.

If these are adaptations to feeling unsafe, they were made deep in the body, in the most fundamental way that it processes the flow of your experience. And the most radical and effective course we can take that addresses root causes is not to adapt to a baseline of threat, but to figure out if we can get safer. Because if we get safer, we change the fundamental neurological calculus of the inputs that are at the root of the flight response driving the anxiety. Get safe and actually register this at an embodied level, and you deprive that engine of fuel. Learn to activate the root drivers of wellbeing autonomically, and you dismantle the engine of anxiety from inside.

We have been taught by a cultural zeitgeist that suggests that we need to go into therapy, and work on our early childhood wounds, and heal them, and develop compassion for ourselves, and for our parents, and have insight into our multi-generational trauma histories, and the epigenetics of trauma, and YES, I grant you, all of this is important. But you can do ALL of this and still not *feel* better. I can understand my own story, why I respond the way I do, have compassion for my parents and the challenges they faced, and for their parents and the limitations they experienced, and for my ancestors and the hardships they endured that hardened them in the ways that

discomfort and pain as teachers, they point us very clearly at precisely what we need to transform.

they were hardened. I can have both insight into all of this, and compassion for everyone, and still feel like shit.

What is making you feel unwell, fundamentally, is that your body has active energy processing templates for experience that are governed by whether or not you feel safe, in danger, or under lifethreat. Your body, right here, right now in this singular present moment. And while the presets for those templates have been written ancestrally, and by your early childhood experiences, the switch on those gates is operated by neural inputs that determine, *in the present moment*, whether we feel safe, in danger, or under lifethreat.

If you cannot flip that switch in the Autonomic Nervous System, none of that other stuff matters.

Yet you don't need a professional intermediary to learn to flip that switch. It is what we are learning to do right here in this book.

Furthermore– as you learn how that switch works, and you start to develop some of the skills that are required to flip it– namely embodied mindful awareness, the ability to self-track your autonomic state, a sense of the total landscape of the autonomic map...it will change nearly every aspect of your life. It will make any work that you do with any mental health professional, body worker, and even physician startlingly more effective. It will dramatically enhance your ability to negotiate relationships. It may also transform your sense of identity, where you are operating from, and how you organize your life. It will likely transform your relationship to your own history.

Most people spend their lives relating to their interior world as though they have about as much control over it as the weather. If they don't like the weather they might self-medicate with alcohol or drugs, or gambling or shopping or by disappearing into a rabbit hole of the internet, or social media, or gaming... they might try to escape the weather by distracting themselves, or going elsewhere, or ignoring it, or resisting it. But to very few people does it occur to directly change the weather.

Those who do wish to change the weather often seek out professional intermediaries. We go consult with professionals to help us interpret the mysterious landscape of our inner worlds, as though they were written in the unreadable scripts of long-dead languages that we cannot read. We go to therapists, and coaches, and astrologers. We call the psychic hotline quietly. We learn to read the enneagram. And don't get me wrong– this is wonderful. Having trusted guides on a journey to awareness is a really really good idea. Understanding ancient knowledge systems– again a really good idea.

But part of what I am trying to tell you here, and which is important for you to recognize and really grasp, is that part of your ability to be well comes from being able to intepret your autonomic landscape from your damn self. This is because you are the one living in your body. And in the same way that having to hand over all of your data to a third-party for interpretation is both cumbersome and inconvenient, you can cut to the chase and learn how your body responds directly. In this, you have an advantage over a health or mental health professional, because you are actually the one wearing your body. Whereas someone who is not wearing your body needs a report about it, needs to engage in asking you questions, needs to do tests, and doesn't know what it has felt like to be you in any moment of your life– all the information you need is available to you simply by learning to listen inwardly to it. It is literally right there, inside you, speaking. It's not even speaking quietly. It is talking all the time. A good deal of the time it is screaming at you. You simply need to learn how to listen to it in its native language, which is a trainable skill, and then you need a map that is clear enough to help you decipher what you are listening to.

For the past thirty years I have been working with an extraordinary team on those maps. They constitute the field of *Autonomics*: the study of the *in vivo* (living) functioning of your

Autonomic Nervous System. The Autonomic Compass on the next page distills thirty years of work into one diagram. Each state is represented by a name, like 'Appease' and a phase of water. The phase of water is pictured in a circle that represents where the state happens on the neuroceptive continuum of safety, danger, or lifethreat. Each state also includes a diagram of a circle filled with triangles. These smaller triangular segments represent the autonomic neurology active in the state.

Blue represents the Connection System. Yellow represents the Movement System. Red represents the Grounding System.

You will notice that the states from 8 o'clock to 12 o'clock, which are health-creating, include all three neurologies, because the coordinating pulsation of safety harnesses the three of them together. You will notice that that states from 1 o'clock to 5 o'clock contain only two triangles: the Connection System triangle is missing. You will notice that the full shutdown state at 6 o'clock contains only the Grounding System neurology, here in its lifethreat configuration. This state is the only time that only a single neurological component of your autonomic neurology is active.

You will also notice that the autonomic mandala is a circle. This is because we can move across and around it in multiple directions. This is hopeful, because it shows us that there are two directions out of every distress state. Previous autonomic models have taught that the only way out of a shutdown state is back through high energy fight or flight states (e.g., from the red at 6 o'clock back to 3 o'clock). Yet we have seen healing lineages from around the world that move people from shutdown back to connection through the doorway of Union and Intimacy.

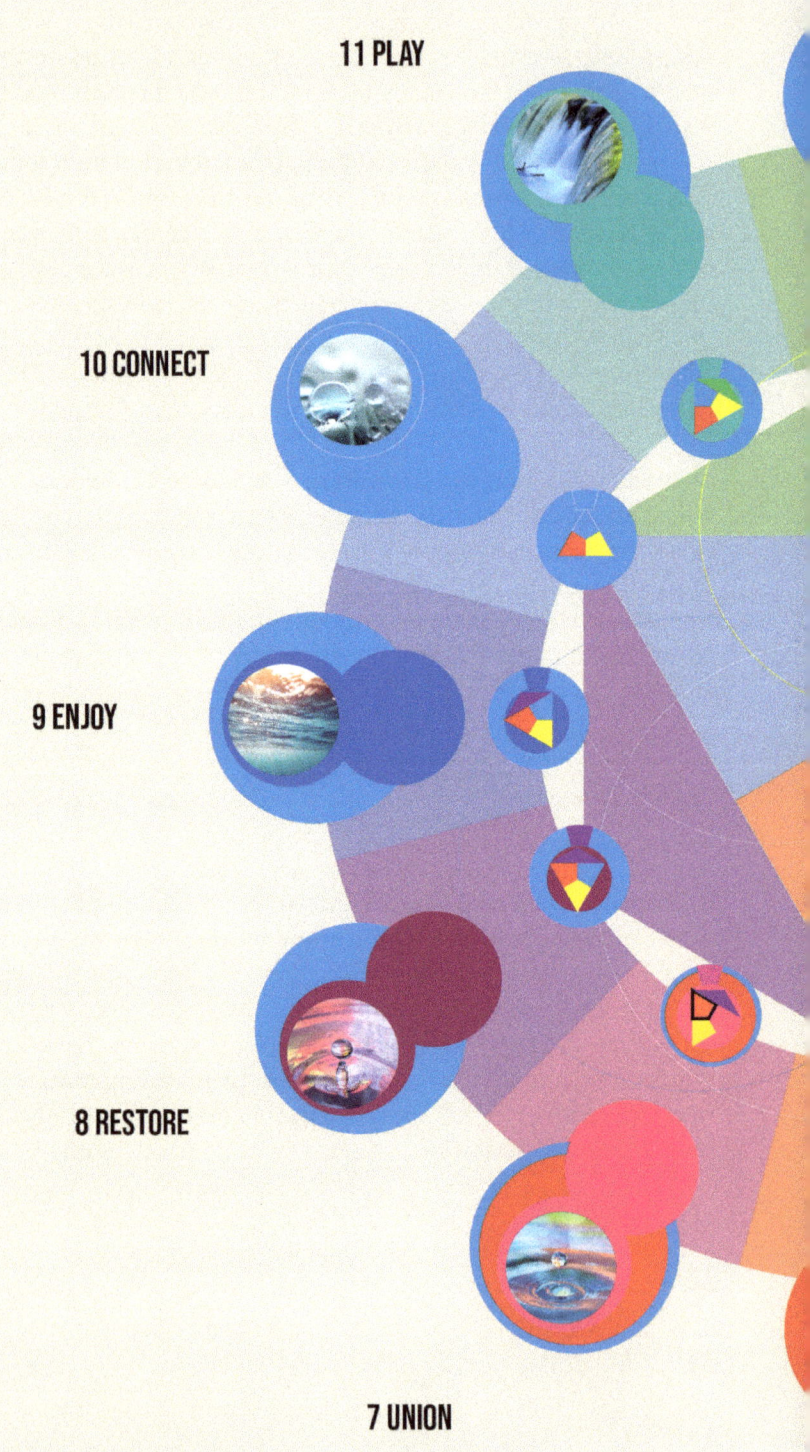

12 COMPETE

11 PLAY

10 CONNECT

9 ENJOY

8 RESTORE

7 UNION

1 ACCOMMODATE

2 APPEASE

3 FIGHT / FLIGHT

4 FREEZE

5 PLACATE

6 SHUTDOWN

The part of ourselves that surfaces autonomic states is not our ordinary sense of self. It is deeper and more primal. This means that there are times in our lives when our bodies will surface a state and our conscious minds do not understand why. We may find ourselves marooned in the wake of an experience, grappling with finding ourselves suddenly stuck in a state that feels distressing and maladaptive (rage, anxiety, overwhelm...), and being utterly unclear how we got there, or how to get out.

The deep neurological calculus driving autonomic state is experiential. Its baselines are sculpted by embodied and felt sense memory of previous experiences. There is a song by Simon and Garfunkel that brings me to tears everytime I listen closely to the words. The song is called *The Boxer*. Paul Simon's voice carries a beautiful vulnerability, but I think the reason the song hits me so hard is that I can see myself in it. It carries for me an element of biography. This is not purely literal; rather it is the description of the title character's story arc. And later in the song is a stanza that kills me everytime I hear it:

In the clearing stands a boxer
and a fighter by his trade
and he carries the reminders
of every glove that laid him down and cut him
til he cried out, in his anger and his shame
Well I am leaving, I am leaving
But the fighter still remains
and still remains...

This fighter, that carries the embodied memory of every glove that has laid you down (everything that has ever really hurt you) is the place from which autonomic decisions arise. The cutting word that freezes your blood and moves your body into sudden winter does so because it reminds your deepest and most elemental sense of self of every time this has happened before. Part of the terror we experience getting shifted into lifethreat states, and danger states, arises from not understanding what they are, or why we feel the way that we do. And it arises because we have been unable to touch the frozen heart of the earlier moments in our lives when we were overwhelmed, suddenly taken from ourselves, and so have not fully metabolized those earlier experiences. It happens because we contain, as adults, the reservoir of ice that remains from every glove that laid us down, every freeze that happened before that we have not thawed in the core of our being. All the inward places that were frozen and abandoned and that we have not been able to touch, and thaw, and reclaim. Suddenly frozen again, suddenly ripped out of ourselves, or bodies having become alien terrain, we are understandably disoriented and bereft. Part of the great power of the autonomic compass is to give us a map and the coordinates for coming back to ourselves, and to teach us, definitively, how to melt that core of ice.

Understanding that the lifethreat state– its innate function– is to immobilize the body, infuse us with endogenous opioids to kill pain and help us dissociate, and that in this state literally nothing feels right, may not make the state any less uncomfortable, but at least we know where we are, and how we got there. Even in alien territory, we know which direction home lies. And the compass has something to tell us about how we can get out of the state. If you find yourself in a foreign landscape where nothing is familiar, the autonomic compass provides the orientation that you need in order to get back home.

Try our interactive Autonomic Compass diagnostics tool by pointing your phone at this QR code.

18- UNLOCKING THE DIAL

Remember that autonomic state is comprised of three elements coming together: neuroception, neurology, and neurochemistry. You can think of these as being sort of like the dials on a combination lock. Autonomic state is what happens when you line up these three dials into a particular sequence.

Autonomic state is on a continuum, another way in which the color spectrum anology is useful. A state can faintly color your experience (slightly irritated) or dominate it with extremely high intensity (enraged). Yet to arise, three elements have to cohere. For the fight state to surface, we have to neurocept danger, get activation chemistry of adrenaline and cortisol onboard, and drop the Connection System such that the Movement and Grounding systems are driving our neurology.

What this alignment also means is that if we are marooned in a state– if we find ourselves swept away into anger, or anxiety, or shutdown, changing any one of the elements can help us unlock the state. I don't want to give you the impression that this is something that you can do in the wake of a serious traumatic injury, but rather that in our movement through the everyday world, understanding this is a very powerful lever to help us have more agency in our autonomic responses to the world, some of which will come upon us and sweep us away.

CHANGE THE NEUROCEPTION

Changing the neuroception of an event means helping our body interpret it differently. The moment I realize that the coiled up snake is actually a garden hose, my neuroception changes. When the two hour wait at the Department of Motor Vehicles starts to seem hilarious to me instead of enraging, I am changing my neuroception. In everyday moments such a reset sometimes happens when we realize that something making us really angry is actually absurd, and we can start to see humor in it.

There is a bit of an art to this, and it is also the dial on the lock where changing our thinking and talking to ourselves (both of which are more top-down strategies) can be most helpful. I know it sounds strange, but there are times when I will address my animal body directly, speaking directly to the neuroceptive elements of this. I might say something like, *Body– I know that this event is freaking you out, and that you are feeling really frightened right now. And I understand why, based on what we've been through, this is making you feel afraid. But here is why I feel that we are going to be 'ok'.* Now, I don't do this unless I believe it to be true. But there are times when I've been able to talk my body down from runaway neuroception of danger.

CHANGING THE CHEMISTRY

When neurochemistry is released, it is going to run its course, which means that ultimately it will be metabolized, and cleared from the body by the kidneys,[1] and eventually excreted through urine. As a general rule, since it's difficult to accelerate the metabolic processing of either activation or shutdown chemistry, a good rule of thumb in terms of alleviating neurochemistry of threat is to try to add oxytocin to the mix. The mechanics of this are variable, because oxytocin doesn't like to release unless you feel safe, but if you can get oxytocin online it can unlock a distress state. In the absence of oxytocin we have fight-flight and overwhelm. Oxytocin can turn nervousness into excitement, and overwhelm into awe. Oxytocin is the chemistry of love and bonding. It can be released by being hugged, intimacy, sexuality. The chemistry of elite performance is adrenaline plus oxytocin. The chemistry of spiritual experience is endogenous opioids and oxytocin. Oxytocin changes the game.

CHANGING THE NEUROLOGY

---

1   There is a glaring exception to this rule the case of lifethreat responses, which I'll address shortly.

Most of the clinical interventions that we have developed are working directly with neurology. The specific ways in which this works breaks out along the lines of state, but the third element that we can work with is bringing online different neurology. We can do this by changing the neural inputs to our systems, as well as by completing self-protective responses, as well as by outflowing stress physiology. We'll go deeper into each of these in the next few chapters, but the idea here is to understand the ways that different threat responses deviate us from access to all autonomic neurology systems, and to work to bring back online the ones that have shifted off. If we are clear about what has been taken offline and why, and how our bodies have processed this shift, we have some agency in shifting this.

The principal idea of this chapter is a framework for under-standing the degree to which each of the elements that com-prise autonomic state can potentially be altered as a gateway to shifting state. It is hopeful news, because it helps us understand that there are multiple ways to help ourselves get unstuck if we find ourselves in an enduring maladaptive state. I want to continue to reiterate here a respect for the manner in which the ANS mediates threat responses. The ANS is a profound embodied intelligence, and the way it responds is meaning-ful. Some states are not better than others. The point is not to valorize Connection states and demonize threat response states. What we are attempting to understand are the root drivers that govern them, why they happen, and how to shift them when and if they are no longer adaptive to the situations we find ourselves in. Enduring threat states are fundamentally incompatible with biological wellbeing.

19- TRANSFORMING FIGHT-FLIGHT STATES

Now let's start looking at specific locations on the autonomic compass. We'll start with fight-or-flight states, which are most people's initial defensive responses.

Because autonomic states are like tuning presets on a stereo, when we get into the nuts and bolts of working with them, we need to understand how the specific preset alters physiological baselines. You have to know whether you are dealing with steam or ice so that you know whether to warm or cool it to bring it back to liquid water. As we look at the more nuanced map of the autonomic compass, we get more specific about understanding each stress state, how it impacts us, and how we can intervene to shift it.

SELF-PROTECTIVE MOTOR RESPONSES

Most distress is a result of us shifting out of safety and connection into threat responses. Yet paradoxically, getting safe doesn't necessarily resolve a threat response, or in and of itself reset the ANS. Take a moment to consider what this means, because it is profound. Let's say that you get news that your boss wants to meet with you during a period when you've been making mistakes at work. Let's say that your immediate embodied response to this is a fear that you are going to lose your job. Let's say that this elicits a flight response (a fear response), which is a pretty natural and adaptational response to this concern.

You steel yourself and go to the meeting, and to your great surprise your boss is actually very supportive. He says he recognizes that you have been having a hard time, and wants you to know he has your back, and has in fact developed a plan to help support you. From outside, it would seem like this news should immediately shift your ANS. *Your concern was unfounded! You're not going to get fired, you are getting more support. How excellent! What a relief.*

The problem, autonomically, is that what resets the ANS is not simply getting safer, but completing self-protective motor movements.

What on earth is a self-protective motor movement?

Your autonomic nervous system is automatic, and it is a system that listens to, and then modulates your organs, often outside of your conscious control or awareness, and whose role is to keep you safe and ensure your survival. The Movement System, which is what we've renamed the spinally-mediated neurology that controls centrally pattern generated movements of the limbs, has all of these deeply ancestrally programmed movement patterns that respond to threat.

There is a whole vocabulary of movements that are universal, and basically hard-wired into your autonomic nervous system. People are doing these movement sequences all the time, we just don't necessarily recognize them.

For example– have you ever been having an argument with someone and they sort of throw up a hand between you, like *Talk to the hand...*

This gesture is actually autonomic. It is a boundary-setting gesture. One of the geeky things that I have been studying, with a whole team of people for the past fifteen years, are classes of similar gestures. Our ANS is hardwired with an entire repertoire of these. They are self-protective in nature, and surfaced by the ANS in response to threat.

So, here's something really interesting. When we go into a fight-or-flight response, and are trying to come out of it, the thing that signals a reset to the body is not simply getting safe, but completing self-protective motor gestures of defense.

WHEN WE ARE TRYING TO COME OUT OF A FIGHT-OR-FLIGHT RESPONSE, THE THING THAT SIGNALS THE ANS TO RESET IS NOT SIMPLY GETTING SAFE, IT IS COMPLETING SELF-PROTEC-TIVE MOTOR GESTURES.

So in the example with your boss, his reassurance is not enough to reset your ANS. You have to complete the self-protective motor gestures of flight.

INNATE MOVEMENT VOCABULARIES

So what is the innate movement vocabulary of defense?

Think about what your body wants to do when you feel in danger and want to flee. Consider for a moment how your body changes. The heart rate elevates, breathing gets fast and shallow, and crucially, your legs power up so that you can get away. Self-protective motor gestures associated with flight typically involve the completion of evasive movements with the legs.

Now, this is not a hard and fast rule. We always want to defer to the individual body and its innate response repertoire. From the lens of autonomic fluency, what we can develop is an ability to listen in a particular way to the movement instincts of our own bodies.

Most of us are socialized since we are very young to over-ride these innate movement signals. We have been trained neurologically to suppress them, and if we aren't good at this we are often told we have problems with impulse control and self-regulation. It's hard to advance in school if we bolt out of the classroom every time we feel afraid, or if we hit every kid in the face when our fight response turns on. But if the body wants to run there is a reason, and if it wants to punch a motherfucker, there's a reason for that as well.

The art of this is to allow the body to complete its unedited responses in a way that doesn't land you in prison. The body has precise and elaborate plans for how it wants to respond to being threatened, and your job, through the lens of autonomic fluency, is to surface these responses so that you can get back to safety without actually endangering others.

If I'm dealing with the boss situation, after the meeting, I will attempt to create a context where I can allow myself to run. What I want to do is get in touch with and allow the impulse to flee to act out. Its impulses need to become physical and translate into movement. I need to tap into the energy of flight and allow my body to successfully get away.

PRACTICE: IF YOU COULD SAY ANYTHING

Since most of us have been trained to suppress our instinctual movement responses, and this lesson is pretty ingrained, when we are working to help people liberate self-protective movement patterns, one of the games we play is called, "If you could say anything..." The premise of the game is simple. We want people to explore how their body would respond if there were no consequences to their actions– if nothing were off limits. We often begin this by asking what they would say in response to a situation that has shifted them into defense. I personally like to do this with people out in the forest, far away from other humans, where yelling is not gonna get the cops called on you. Once someone realizes I'm serious, and sometimes I have to model this for them, which I like to do with the inclusion of a few choice F-bombs at high volume, I can usually get the person to verbalize their discomfort pretty good.

Yet what I'm watching for are the movements of the body as they begin to let go of holding themselves back, and that is what I help them *feel*. Self-protective responses connected to fight generally involve the arms and hands, those of flight generally involve the legs and feet. You may be surprised by how specific the body's agenda is. I was working with a client who was very mild-mannered, in her late sixties, and we were working on some very primal, very early self-protective responses from the time she was maybe six years old. When she really allowed herself to get into it, she delivered a stunning death blow to the back of the neck with a precision her ordinary sense of self could not have managed, scooted me across the floor and kicked me into the fire with great precision and relish. Very specific gestures.

20- WORKING WITH WHAT ARISES

I realized this morning, at about 4 am, that my family may need to move. I recognize now, writing this sentence, that the word *move* is the action indicated. This awareness was something that had been building in me, with significant discomfort, for about a month. It is the result of several situations that are outside of our control, but that in aggregate may change our calculus on living in the place where we currently reside.

I wouldn't necessarily have chosen this timing, if it were up to me. But life often isn't up to us. As they say, *You cannot stop the waves, but you can learn to surf.* When I sat down at my computer to write this morning, my body simply said, *No.* In order to write, I have to feel settled. I have to be able to listen inwardly, and the level of tumult I was experiencing made this impossible. Instead, I went downstairs, spent a few minutes listening inwardly, and felt that what my body wanted to do was run around like a crazy person, flapping my arms in useless panic. Strangely, simply visualizing myself doing this (which touched into the neurological movement *impulse*) was enough to make me vomit. I got up from the couch where I was sitting, went into the bathroom, and threw up in a few crisp heaves.

My rational mind can find no real utility in flapping my arms around in the air like a panicked toddler, but the part of my awareness that was responding to the news that we might need to move is not my rational mind. And this part of myself, for whatever reason, had a very specific set of movement needs that, once I allowed myself to begin to move my arms in this manner, continued to cause me to need to vomit. Let me set the record straight here. This is not a movement I can remember making ever in my life. I do remember seeing my daughter, when she was about two years old, making a somewhat similar movement when she was distressed, but this was more spastic than what she did. I did not select it from the repertoire of gestures that Gabriel likes to make. Running around like someone panicking because their hair is on fire is something my body chose. What I permitted, rather than suppressing, was for this movement pattern to make its way up into motion. Once I had done this for several minutes, I found myself in a totally different autonomic landscape. My body had moved itself from distress at the edge of panic to a very different state.

I then sat down and made an inventory of every item in our house, because when I looked up 'steps to prepare for moving' it was one of the first things listed, and it occurred to me it would be useful for both organization and insurance purposes. I am writing this chapter much later in the day. Prior to sitting down to write, my wife and I had a fairly intense argument (*I'm sure it was really fun for her to encounter me talking about this first thing this morning*), during which we rehashed the past six years of our marriage, composting a set of decisions that irked her and made her resentful and have for several years, trying to find common ground, trying to find our way into a shared course of action. We traveled (at different times) from exasperation to resentment to anger to indignation through attempts at mutual coercion with one another, before settling into a detente, before being able to really listen to one another with empathy and understanding. Later in the afternoon we went to look at houses, ate lunch together, and then held hands.

Now I'm writing this. The intelligence of my ANS this morning was to require a freak-out, and then demand action. Both the freak-out and the demand for action were catalyzed by my aptly named Movement System, which needed to first flap its arms like a dizzy flightless bird, and then organize a set of actions. The feeling that we have that we need to *do something* is a manifestation of this need to act.

Does this ever happen to you? A sudden need to take action, where sitting still feels just terrible?

Since most modern people spend a good deal of their time running around like chickens with their heads cut off, *doing*

doing doing, we've heard a lot in some circles since the modern mindfulness movement gathered steam: *Don't do something, just sit there.* And while this tilt toward inward listening, feeling, and introspection is tremendously useful, that is only so if your ANS is on board with it.

Here's a secret: the way your attention works is downstream of your autonomic state. That is because autonomics governs your survival, so it is at the top of your biological priority list. Attention is in service to your survival. As is every other feature of your biology. So if your autonomic state wants you be able to sit still, this will work. And if it does not, good luck. If you force it to sit still– and lots of meditators are very good at this– you will move into a dissociative state. Just to be clear, you are no longer meditating then, you are detaching. And that is not what the Buddha meant when he was talking about non-attachment.

Autonomic fluency means listening in at the level of your survival responses, and learning to honor the demands they are making of your system, with the recognition that there is intelligence in the demands. When we try to override the ANS, we lose. Had I forced myself to sit down and write this morning, I would likely have pushed myself into dissociation, because my sovereign body was not on board with this.

Most of us have been trained, in a crisis, to double-down on thinking, but I would like to challenge this. When we are shifting into defense, when we are shutting down, prioritizing thinking is likely to push us further out of our bodies, further away from groundedness, farther away from the rhythms of breath and body.

PRACTICE: MOVE LIKE YOU

My editor did not like the previous title of this exercise: *Move like the weirdo that you are.* Trying to be helpful, I was like, "How about, *Move like the freak that you are?*" All of us, since we are young, have been socialized to be self-conscious of the ways that we move. We are way too concerned with looking cool. This training is rarely explicit, but it is pervasive. If we have grown up in the United States, with its celebrity-worshipping culture, we have been schooled all of our lives in the art of careless cool, and many of us find it difficult to move authentically because we have been trained to be self-conscious of our gestures, our postures. We have been taught to be aware of how we look, how we move, not from a sense of inwardness – how it feels to us inside – but from appearance, as outsiders looking in, watching ourselves as others may see us. Autonomically, this translates into inhibition on movements that don't look or feel *ok* to us. So flapping my arms like someone whose hair has caught on fire? Not cool, therefore not ok, therefore I'm not gonna do it. But your ANS doesn't care whether or not the way you move is cool. So we want to reclaim all manner of unorthodox movement in the service of liberation. How do you move when you know no one is watching? What are the gestural repertoires that your body wishes to express innately, but that you do not give yourself permission to express? Can you move like the singular animal that you are?

21- IN THE NERVOUS SYSTEM, NOT THE EVENT

Often in the world of trauma healing, you will hear that trauma is in the nervous system, not the event. What this means is that our individual deep nervous systems (the ANS), and how they interpret what is happening to us are the key variable in determining how we will respond to an event. What is terrifying for one person is exhilarating for someone else. To someone who hates public speaking, giving a public talk feels like jumping out of a plane, while to a skydiver, jumping out of a plane feels like giving a great public talk. Some people ride rollercoasters and watch scary movies for fun. Other people couldn't be paid to do either one.

In the image on the facing page, the two young people in the first car, getting ready to plunge, are eyes closed and wincing. The boy on the right with his mouth open is definitely making noise. The woman in the third car, however, looks quite relaxed. This might be because her car hasn't gotten sucked into the gravity vortex of the slope, so she cannot yet feel its pull, or it might be how she rides. Whether you are like the riders in the first car or the third, autonomic fluency is knowing how your deep nervous system responds to life, and using this information and the vital energies the ANS drives through us to help you live your best life.

The context, what it means to us, how our bodies interpret the situation, what we have endured in our lives– all of these factors come together to sculpt our neural interpretation of what is happening. We need to become aware of our unique autonomic landscape, and how it sculpts the way that we interact with the world. Once we begin to know this, and to work with it consciously, we can learn to expand the range of what experiences we can pass through while holding onto enough safety to keep our Connection Systems online and stay available and open to experience. And in tandem, we can learn how to collaborate with the ANS and support its digestion of danger and lifethreat responses so that we learn from them and move through them. We can develop the skills to more actively digest difficult experiences.

Understanding the way that autonomic state comes together through neuroception, neurology, and chemistry is such a powerful framework for working intentionally with autonomic responses. Recognizing this reality gives me three distinct levers to work if and when the ANS surfaces responses that feel maladaptive, or keep me stuck in defense. Armed with this insight, I can work with my own body and nervous system and its particular history with more compassion, patience, and skill. Decoupled from context and meaning-making, the neurology and chemistry of nervousness and excitement are identical. What colors it one way or the other is our interpretation of the event. Learning to work with, not against the strong energies evoked by the ANS orients into collaborating with our deepest survival intelligence, rather than resisting it, which doesn't work anyway.

22- WORKING WITH SHUTDOWN

Surely shutdown is the most uncomfortable and intrinsically distressing of the threat responses. It is the one that makes us feel most alien to ourselves– its transformations of our interiority most startling, severe, and unfathomable.

Shutdown is our body's response to impending lifethreat, so to get here the ANS has to detect that we are in extraordinary danger. When this happens– and it can occur gradually or suddenly– we lose two of the three autonomic systems that ideally undergird our experience. First, we lose the Connection System that coordinates face, heart, and hands, underpinning our *relating*. Then, we lose the Movement System, which coordinates complex patterned movement, undergirding *action*. Absent these two systems, unable to relate to the experience, or act in response to it, we are left with only our Grounding System, but in its traumatic configuration, which is generally an immobilization response.

This neurology, which is largely organized in the guts, leaves us in a state of collapse. Our bodies fall inward, we lose the tone of our core, our pelvic floor, our backs slump, our chests cave in. We literally cannot hold ourselves up. This neurological collapse is twinned with the arrival of endogenous opioids which, if strong enough, move us into a landscape of surreality. Given that the drivers of this response are usually terror-inducing, the dream landscape is generally one of horror. Suddenly our bodies are impinged upon by strange sensations or their utter lack, and we are marooned far from our ordinary sense of self, in nightmarish circumstances, unable to activate the neural circuits whereby we ordinarily feel, sense, and know ourselves.

One of the most challenging things about working with shutdown is not freaking out, because the state when truly activated feels so bad. From within it– an ice state– we do not have access to everyday cognition or problem-solving, so we find

ourselves beside ourselves, and yet unable to muster the awareness to figure out how to fix this. Yet shutdown is a state with
its own logic, and so let's parse it so that we can help you find
the trail of breadcrumbs to make your way home should you
get stranded here.

I'm going to treat the next section on working with shutdown
as though something has happened that has shifted you into
this state, but you are no longer in acute emergency. From
within emergency, we do not have the conditions to exit such
a state. Yet like other defensive states, simply getting back to
safety does not necessarily shift us out of this state. Rather, the
next section supposes that you recognize that your ANS has
shifted into a shutdown response, but that are out of the acute
danger phase and rather in its aftermath. A final note here: like
all autonomic states, shutdown operates on a continuum. At
the low end, where it is faintly humming in the background,
this might involve feeling spacey or forgetful. At high intensity
it involves dissociation, numbness, depression, and de-person-
aliziation or de-realization.

SHUTDOWN IS AN OVERWHELM STATE

Shutdown is an overwhelm state. We get truly hijacked by it
when we cannot process our experience. There is too much
information incoming too fast, and we do not have the neurological bandwidth to make sense of it. Shutdown is overwhelm.

DECREASE THE INFORMATION INCOMING

Once we understand this fundamental truth, we can become
more compassionate with ourselves by dramatically restricting
the amount of information that is incoming. We want an environment with minimal stimulation. Quiet. No demands on our
nervous system. Not a lot of people, not a lot of activity. We
don't want people asking us a lot of questions. We also might
not want to be alone, which can create a bit of a problem. We
don't want a lot of eye contact. Stimulation is overwhelming

in this state. If someone is with you therefore, they should be non-demanding, parallel to you physically (as opposed to facing you), not looming over, but at your height, and simply present. Think of being seated together in the fronts seats of a car, looking out over the ocean. They are sort of parallel, doing their thing, not making demands on you. (If you are present with someone in a shutdown state, this is also how you'd want to be present with them. It is extremely unlikely that they will have the presence of mind to be able to communicate this to you, so you can just simply know it, and do it.)

DON'T TRY TO DO ANYTHING

Paradoxical as it sounds, the best way to exit a shutdown state is by not trying to do anything to exit a shutdown state. The goal is to find our way back to the present moment. Active 'doing' will not accomplish this. You cannot force it.

TRADITIONAL MINDFULNESS PRACTICE IS CONTRA-INDICATED

At a visceral level, shutdown is almost always accompanied by a feeling of vacancy in the guts. This may feel like a bowling ball in your belly, or a void. There will be some parts of the body that go offline; that are simply inaccessible. Because attention potentiates experience (turns up the dial on whatever we are attending to) bringing your attention to parts of the body that are vacant will increase your experience of dissociation. This is why traditional inwardly-oriented mindfulness practice is HIGHLY CONTRA-INDICATED in shutdown. I sincerely wish more mindfulness teachers understood this.

FIND THE EDGE OF SENSATION

Instead, if you are listening inwardly, find the edges of the shutdown in the body. Find the places on the edge of the absences in your body where there are flickers of sensation. Attend to the sensations of the edges without getting sucked into the center. Work at the border of these sensations, sensing, feeling, sense-making with what arises. Work at the threshold, in the liminal states at the edges. Fragments of memory, emotion, and sensation are likely to emerge, swarm together, and begin to organize. Let yourself feel the visceral discomfort. Let your body move, adjust, squirm as needed. Trust any unusual movement impulses that arise, let them carry out.

FEED SAFETY INTO THE EXTREMITIES

By changing neural inputs to the hands, the feet, and the skin, we can work against the gravity of shutdown in the core. Getting your feet on the earth, getting something with a pleasing texture into your hands, wrapping yourself in a blanket, taking a hot shower, feeling sunlight on your skin...all of these are gentle ways of increasing the visceral inputs of safety at the edges (periphery) of the body. Since sensory systems feed inward and upward, changing conditions at the perimeter helps to thaw the core.

INHIBITION ON BREATH

When you are in a shutdown state, the body suppresses the breath. As uncomfortable as this feels, it is not a cause for alarm. It is simply a function of the state. The origin of the state is very very ancient, and is connected to a diving reflex that shuts down the breath. Even though you cannot breathe, there is nothing wrong with your breath, or with your lungs. Yes, you cannot breathe normally. No, this is not an additional cause for concern.

Instead of fighting with this, see if you can allow the breath to stop if it wants to, and see if you can allow the body to find its innate desire to breathe through the language of sensation. As uncomfortable as this is, and while this suppression of breath and concomitant plunge in heartrate can kill a pre-term infant[11], I'm not aware of adults ever dying from this. I once

---

1 Just to be crystal clear about this, if you were ever in a situation where you were with a baby who went into this state, then not

experienced my breath hold itself for about four minutes (I'm saying that my breath held itself because this is far far longer than the longest I've ever held my breath on purpose) when I was coming out of a deep shutdown state. If we can have an attitude of curiosity toward this (have confidence that you are not going to die) rather than freaking out and setting your hair on fire (*Oh my God!!! I'm not breathing– what the fuck is wrong with me???*) you will have a totally different experience of this. The hold on breath is intimately linked to the dissociative process. Its return is intimately linked to coming back into our bodies. The place where you can actually touch the absence of breath is the place where it is just about to reorganize. Consider this a kind of profound awareness practice of stretching into extreme discomfort.

HEAD AND NECK

I probably should have addressed this earlier, when we were talking about fight-or-flight responses, because it applies to the entire continuum of defensive states. When we are in a connection state, and are feeling safe and available, the curvature of the head and neck where they junction is the classical sort of arc that you see in diagrams of the human spine. This allows the head to move freely on the neck, with full rotational range and ease. When there is a threat, and our eyes are focalizing a danger signal, this curvature goes away. The alteration of the rotation of the atlas and axis, the first and second cervical vertebrae, reduces bloodflow to cranial nerves. We can experience this as fixity in the neck/head junction, tension, and constriction that can feel very mechanical, yet is also neurological. So the way the head balances on the spine changes.

This effects our sense of balance and the organization of the body in space. Knowing this, one of the things that you can do very gently is to lay down on your back with a rolled-up towel under your neck, and see if you can sort of allow the curvature

---

breathing is a very serious problem. You, however, are not a baby and your neurology is very different.

of the neck to reintroduce. Don't force this; don't DO anything. But the way the head is moving in relationship to the spine has a deep impact on how we feel in our bodies, and so supporting restoration here can have big positive impacts on how we feel.

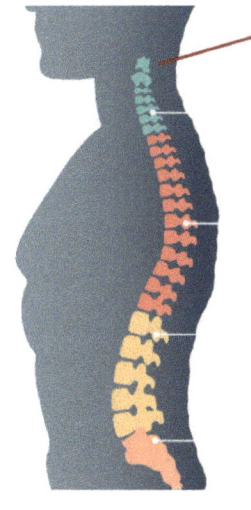

THIS RED LINE POINTS TO THE JUNCTION OF THE ATLAS AND AXIS WITH THE SPINE.

At this junction, during stress responses, the angle of the head on the neck changes, compressing bloodflow to cranial nerves and restricting range of movement in the head. Sometimes it does not re-organize. Gentle support to re-introduce the arc and process the movement constriction can be very relieving.

CORE IS NOT AVAILABLE

One of the most fundamental attributes of shutdown states is losing contact with sensation in the unmyelinated vagus beneath the respiratory diaphragm, e.g., in the guts. If you get shifted into shutdown, you will typically notice that your ability to feel yourself in the deep belly is compromised. The kind of core work that we do in Pilates, or that is required for sit-ups? These deep intrinsic muscles of the viscera go offline. The pelvic floor goes offline. So another practice is to keep trying to find access to those muscles again. Do not force this, do not try to do anything, but see if you can find and feel them again. Same with the pelvic floor. Work from the edges toward the center. Finding our way back to sensation in these areas, by mechanically contracting and releasing them, can be a way to begin to return to sensation and shift the state.

SHAKING

Although it looks inert from outside, the shutdown state is like trapping a hurricane in a bottle. It contains extraordinarily high levels of activation. As these begin to metabolize, the body may shake. While shaking is not the point, not the end goal, it is a manifestation of energy metabolizing. There are a number of trauma-healing modalities that make shaking an explicit part of their pedagogy. These include Somatic Experiencing, developed by Dr. Peter Levine, and TRE (Trauma Release Exercise) developed by Dr. David Bercelli.

FEET ON THE GROUND

If you are shaking, its a good idea to get your feet on the ground. Give the energy back to the earth. She will help you metabolize it. Think of grounding an electrical circuit.

ROME WAS NOT DESTROYED IN A DAY

At the beginning of this book, in the author's note, I said that if you are a modern person you are traumatized. I stand by this. If you are now getting a sense of how to transform a shutdown response, I can also assure you that this is not the first time you've gone into shutdown in your life. What this means, at a very practical level, is that you have an accumulation of shutdown energy, probably from the time that you were very small. One of the most fascinating things that we have discovered is that most people have a great deal of archived shutdown response in their bodies. I think it is difficult for many of us to understand exactly how much allostatic load we have learned to carry. Like frogs who have been slowly boiled all of our lives, we are usually just not aware of how hot the water we have been swimming in is until our health starts to degrade.

If you had met me twenty years ago, you might have thought I was an asshole, but you would not have been aware of the degree to which my body had archived an extraordinary trauma load. I was, at the time, barely aware of this myself. I want to explain to you that the body I am wearing has changed dramatically over the past decade as my own inner archeology and trauma healing has proceeded. When I graduated highschool I weighed 135 pounds. Today, I weight 180. About 40 pounds of that are muscle. My body as a young person was so acutely tensioned by the amount of trauma it was carrying that I literally could not put on mass. I lifted weights and worked out feverishly at times in my twenties, without ever gaining weight. I spent decades with undiagnosable gastro-intestinal distress, and no medical practitioner I ever worked with was able to link it to the degree of shutdown response my body was residing in. I suffered multiple bouts of depression as well, and again no one was able to link this to the ANS.

The way it feels to be me, living in my body, has changed completely in the past 15 years. Because over this time I have thawed a great deal of ice. One of the things I have found most suprising, as well as most hopeful, about the transformation of shutdown, is that endogenous opioids endure in your system until they are metabolized. This means that shutdown responses from fifty years ago have an enduring chemical signature that is still in your body. I know this intimately from my own experience, and I know it from clinical work that we have done with hundreds of patients and clients with whom I've worked individually.[2]

The road to transforming your historical archive of shutdown is likely long, but if you find that you are prone to moving into shutdown, it is a good indicator of this kind of accumulation. I would encourage you to seek out specialized support for this from a trained somatically-oriented trauma therapist. These therapies will not be talk-based, but rather bottom-up and

---

2 We have worked with tens of thousands of people around the world. I have worked in one-on-one sessions clinically with a selection of them, probably several hundred people who have come to us for consultation and support around complex neurological dysfunction, often having worked unsuccessfully with multiple neurologists, occupational therapists, physical therapists, etc.

body-based, and will help you to exit long-stagnant accumulations of allostatic load. You may be astounded by how much life improves.

OXYTOCIN

There is an enduringly false impression in a number of trauma healing modalities that the only exit from shutdown states is by going back into high-energy fight-or-flight states. This has become part of the prevailing orthodoxy in somatic trauma healing. This misapprehension arises from a number of factors, including that most stress research is done on white men.

In our experience it is true that if you entered a shutdown state by going through the roof of fight-or-flight, exiting a shutdown state will likely bring you back into the fight-or-flight state that preceded it. This is an important thing to understand because it means that sometimes, when someone is healing from shutdown states, as they are healing they will shift back into very high-energy fight-or-flight states. What this feels like is moving from numbness, indifference, or dissociation into extreme states of either rage or terror. If you are feeling rage or terror, you are no longer in shutdown, because shutdown is by definition immobilized and flat of affect.

If this happens to people and they don't understand why, even though it is an improvement autonomically (your Movement System just came back online, now you have two autonomic systems available), it doesn't *feel* like an improvement. So there is some wisdom in knowing that if you got to shutdown through fight-or-flight, you will likely pass back through it when you exit. If this happens, and you are supporting someone, you would move from applying the principles used to transform shutdown states that you are reading about now to the principles used to transform fight-or-flight states a couple of chapters previous.

Yet it is also the case that there is another pathway out of shutdown that is more matrilineal, and involves moving directly from shutdown back to connection. Think of this as passing directly from ice to liquid water, rather than ice to steam to liquid water. This pathway is applicable if you went into shutdown directly, as in moving from an ordinary state straight into shutdown. What these matrilineal and medicine pathways have in common (we have discovered such traditions in Brazil and other ancestral and indigenous cultures) is that they leverage intimacy. At a chemical level, this takes the form of introducing oxytocin. Oxytocin is the chemistry of love and bonding. Some of these traditions literally make use of being held, where the person working to transform shutdown is literally cradled in someone else's arms. Some of them involve other botanicals or chemical compounds (MDMA, entheogens, empathogens, etc.) that help shift the nervous system into a deep sense of safety, from which endogenous oxytocin production can exhibit a transforming effect on the shutdown state.

If you consider the chemistry of sexuality, you will notice that one way of describing physical intimacy between lovers is *immobilization without fear.* Oxytocin can be used to mediate this transition from immobilization with fear (shutdown) to immobilization without fear.

23- THE CONTINUUM OF APPEASE

Imagine for a moment that you are negotiating with your boss for a higher salary. You want a particular outcome here, and at some level you are fighting for this. But if you shift into a full-fledged fight response, and go into attack mode, putting your boss on the defensive, you are not likely to achieve the outcome you desire. So when you negotiate, you utilize elements of sociality, while at the same time having to marshall fight energy in constructive ways. This is an example of the kinds of energies that co-exist in the continuum that stretches from negotiating to appeasing to placating.

Negotiating is not comfortable. It takes effort to balance between being social and combative. Keeping your boss calm enough to feel met and possibly appreciated, while asserting your own value and advocating for something that you want? These two energies don't typically mix easily. Being deferential and assertive at the same time? Not easy. Yet negotiating is on the subtle end of the appeasing continuum because at least here the two impulses are not fully in opposition. Full-fledged appeasing happens when our bodies are feeling under threat (in danger or lifethreat) but we use sociality to make ourselves safer.

In order to be able to do this, we have to turn down our awareness of the inward sense of danger. This is generally accomplished by turning attention outward, and putting it on the person that we are trying to appease. This provides a deeper sense of safety, because typically they are the source of the danger. Having our attention focused on them keeps the danger visible to us. Yet the cost of this outward focus is that we are not in contact, inwardly, with our experience of threat. And the re-inforcement of this habit is that when we feel in danger, rather than bringing our attention inward, rather than focusing on what we feel and what we need, we focus on trying to change something (or someone) in the outer world.

There is nothing intrinsically wrong with the appease response, just as there is nothing intrinsically wrong with any defensive response. It becomes problematic when it becomes automatic, and when it becomes maladaptive to context. Our goal in autonomic fluency is to have a full menu of adaptive defensive responses, and to be able to match them to the situations we find ourselves in.

There are times when appeasing is an effective and appropriate response: we wouldn't do it if it didn't work. There is also a direct relationship between appeasing and developing autoimmune issues. Why is this? The immune system is, fundamentally, a system whose purpose is to distinguish Self from Other. In order to identify what is us, and what is not us, it develops a very nuanced and elaborate chemical recognition of who we are. This is what permits it to detect intrusion. Appeasing, if practiced long and deeply enough, denatures our awareness of the difference between self and other. It teaches us to orient outward to the experience of someone else, rather than inward to our own innate needs and responses. In the absence of this direct inward contact with our own interiority, we lose a sense of who we actually are, sometimes even at an existential level.

The continuum of appease has not been part of the classical map of defensive responses, but this is because most stress research in the United States has been done by straight white men on straight white men, and as a demographic straight white men are the least likely to display this defensive response, because when your social location is centered, when you are atop the hierarchy of white supremacy and patriarchy and hetero-normativity, appeasing is not required as frequently. Yet in our work with clients in fifty countries internationally, we see appeasing behaviors with the same frequency we see fight, flight, and shutdown responses. They are fundamental to how human nervous systems cope with being enmeshed in a domination paradigm.

Appeasing is defined by a neuroception of danger, paired with a neurological response that co-opts sociality while the under-lying neurology is defensive (steam or ice). When the underlying defensive response is a fight-or-flight response (steam), we call this appeasing. When the underlying defensive response is a shutdown response (ice), we call this placating. Both of these behavioral repertoires have been trained into people who have been subjugated, because talking back to the Emperor will get you killed.

Appeasing is something that we often learn early in life. Beyond the fundamental mechanics of subjugation, it is the province of middle children, peace-makers, folks who grow up in families where there is upheaval. It is also often trained into girls and women, where it is normalized (the archetype of the tradwife is a normalization of appeasing as virtue)[1].

A sensitive child can discern, pretty early on, and pretty intui-tively, that they can use their own body as a sort of capacitor to absorb conflict in a family. We can learn to spread ourselves out between people, across conflict and difficulty, and absorb it. Sometimes children learn to do it by being funny. Sometimes children learn to do it by sacrificing their own health, and becoming a family-designated patient. Taking care of them becomes something the family can unite around. Often these self-sacrificing choices are made outside of conscious aware-ness, which makes these habits hard to change. We can become so adept at this that we don't realize we are doing it.

Like any autonomic state, any energy-processing template, there are times when appeasing is an adaptive behavior, and

---

1   The domination paradigm of patriarchy, that plays out through the notion that the father is the 'head of the household' is an entire social construction designed to de-center the sovereignty of women. Women's role in this construct is predicated on their willingness to appease domineering men. Tradwives are supposed to embrace this subjugation. When women's bodies become repositories for the toxic energies of men, they become sick. (When anyone's bodies become repositories for the toxic energies of anyone else, they become sick.) When a cultural or religious system trains you to do this, you should take a good hard look at who it is benefiting.

there are times when it becomes maladaptive. Our goal, with autonomic fluency, is to have the full repertoire of autonomic responses available to us: to have all responses on the menu, and not to fall into a particular defensive response simply because it is a habit. We want to be able to respond appropriately to what the situation we are experiencing demands. Often people begin to realize that they are exhibiting appeasing behaviors because their health begins to fail. There is a high correlation between appeasing as your defensive response of choice and auto-immune issues, cancer, chronic illness, fibromyalgia, migraines...

Part of the reason we can get sick from appeasing is that we are absorbing other people's high-intensity energy. If there is conflict, and I feel in danger, the simplest and most innate response is to set a boundary (fight response) or get away (flight response). Since connection makes us vulnerable, when aggression is directed at us, it feels better if we create a boundary so that we are less available to the feelings of harm that come from being aggressed, or escape. Staying open to having aggression directed at you is painful, emotionally if not outright physically.

Think about watching animals in the wild. If two big cats are getting ready to fight, you see a lot of high-intensity behavior, but you will almost never see one animal try to talk the other out of being upset. Shelley Taylor, a Professor at UCLA who coined the term 'tend-and-befriend', envisions the social origins of this response in early human mothers with children who were dealing with a violent mate. The mother cannot fight off the mate because if she is harmed, it reduces the likelihood the children will survive. So *fight* comes off the table as an adaptive response. Nor can she pick up the children and escape with them; she won't be able to run fast enough to get away. *Flight* comes off the table. She doesn't have the luxury of shutting down, because she won't be able to attend to them. *Shutdown* is off the table. So what does she do? Turns toward the mate and attempts to calm him down. Tries to disarm him with sociality. There is a full repertoire of behaviors that might be necessary to accomplish this, depending on how angry (or drunk) he is.

Allopathic medicine is terrible at diagnosing and treating stress-related disorders generally, but it is particularly awful at diagnosing and treating stress-related disorders that arise out of the appeasing continuum, because it doesn't recognize appeasing as a universal stress response.

You know that you are exhibiting appeasing behavior if you find yourself wanting to avoid conflict, trying to people-please, wishing everyone would just get along. Or if you find yourself being nicer to other people when you are upset with them than you intend to. Or if it is difficult to say NO, set a boundary, or defend yourself against other people's incoming energy. [2]

---

2   Permeability to incoming energy is a hallmark of shutdown chemistry, so it can also be a result of being in shutdown. Placating is the form of appeasing where sociality is blended over a shutdown response.

24- TRANSFORMING THE APPEASE RESPONSE

Let's map out a pathway here for exploring how to transform habitual patterns of appeasing. The prelimary phases of learning how to transform this response require a good deal of work with awareness. Often people who are habitually appeasing really do not know that they are doing this. It has become habitual to a degree that they do not feel it.

We cannot change a behavior that we are not aware of, so the first step in transforming the response is to begin to recognize when you are doing it. And because you are likely doing it automatically, this is not easy.

BUILDING AWARENESS OF THE PATTERN

There are, however, some pretty telltale signs that you are appeasing. For example

- having difficulty directly communicating your needs
- being nicer to people than you feel that you want to be, particularly when you are upset with them
- being nice to people's faces and then accumulating resentment about it
- finding yourself wishing that everyone would just get along
- taking better care of other people than you are taking care of yourself
- engaging in relationships that feel asymmetrical for long periods of time[3]
- feeling depleted by your relationships
- having to always 'talk someone down'

---

3 Clearly there are some relationships that are asymmetrical by design. Parenting a child is asymmetrical. Mentoring someone is asymmetrical. What I'm talking about here are friendships or partnerships where there are long-stranding emotional asymmetries.

If you are appeasing, at the level of your moment-to-moment attention, you will notice that when you are in-the-moment relating with someone and engaging this behavior, it will be easier for you to attend to them– i.e., their energy, gesture, posture, facial expression, emotionality– than to feel yourself. This is a really important clue to transforming this behavior.

Generally speaking, our attention can either rest inwardly (such as when we are doing a bodyscan), outwardly (such as when we are looking at something), or on the relational field, which holds both. If you find that you are relating with someone, and the majority of your attention is on them– e.g., if you find that tracking them is more available to you than tracking yourself inwardly, it is a good indicator that you are doing some appeasing.

Did I just describe being a mother? Possibly. Should it feel like this when you are parenting small children? Probably. Is this an indicator of appeasing when you are doing it with other adults? Absolutely.

DISRUPTION OF RELATIONSHIPS

At the outset, let's note that altering appeasing behavior is likely to disrupt your relationships, because appeasing is essentially the activity of metabolizing the energy of other people for them. If you do this habitually, then the people you are in relationship with are used to you eating their waste energy, and if you stop doing this they will notice immediately.

Let's also notice how socially normalized this behavior is, particularly for women. There are a lot of ideas in our society about men being less capable of parsing their emotions, or dealing with emotion in general. Women often play the role of emotional whisperers for men, helping them to figure out what they are feeling, helping them to respond emotionally in ways that are appropriate. This often results in women absorbing toxic energy from men, which is what we are talking about. The real solution to this problem is for men to become more adept at metabolizing their own emotions, not for women to do it for them.

What you need to prepare for, as you undertake this transformational work, is that it will give rise to new negotiations of personal and energetic boundaries, and personal and energetic space. If the people you are in relationship with are unwilling to change and grow and alter the way that they are interacting with you, the relationships will likely reach a breakpoint.

Let's stop right there, and notice how this lands with you. The appeasing reponse, because it directly involves managing and metabolizing the energy of others, is directly woven into the fabric of relational contact. Can you feel that?

It is not abstract at all. We are talking about the ways that we touch one another energetically as animals. If one person is absorbing excess or toxic energies that another person cannot metabolize themselves, and the person absorbing those energies stops doing it, the person emitting the energies immediately feels this because they will feel worse. There is no delay. They feel it immediately.

This can create extreme awkwardness, specifically because appeasing is a subjugation response, and the person in the dominant position feels it when the person in the subjucated position stops accepting being subjugated. When we stop appeasing, we alter the felt texture of relationship immediately. The person used to dominating will not know what has happened. They will experience a sense of suddenly being constrained, or contained, or diminished. They will feel like their emotional territory has inexplicably shrunk.

NOTICING

The first step in transforming appeasing responses is to notice when you are engaged in appeasing. Appeasing is a relational habit, so we do it in the context of relating to others. You can ask yourself:

-How can I tell that I am appeasing?

-How does it feel in the body?

Notice it in the body. When are you, in conflict, absorbing the energy of others? There is a bodyset to this. What is the gap between what you are expressing and what you are feeling? When you first start to sense into this, it is likely to feel murky. You are bringing discernment to separate the strands of a response that have been conjoined.

DISCERN THE COMPONENTS

You may need to move your attention intentionally back-and-forth from what you are doing (accommodating) to the underlying internal distress energy you are experiencing. It is important for you to discern if the underlying inward experience is one of something on the fight continuum, something on the flight continuum, or shutdown. In the first case you are likely to notice some version of irritation, in the second some version of anxiety, in the third some sense of going away: a loss of self.

In the same way that we might realize we are stressed out because we find ourselves eating chocolate (the chocolate is not the problem, it is the solution), we can recognize appease as the solution to the deeper problem of feeling unsafe, and try to bring our attention back to the foundation layer of the felt sense of danger. This felt sense will guide you– once you are clearer about whether your response is a fight, flight, or shutdown reponse, you are now clearer about the primary signal in your body.

Take time to see if you can allow yourself to tolerate this signal. Often we stop feeling that primary signal because it is too uncomfortable. Often this is behavior that originates in early childhood, and has to do with deep layers of the environments in which we were raised. It is worth taking time with this, because you are now in contact with the root of the signal that appeasing has been developed to overcome. Can you remember when you determined that this initial danger signal was intolerable to feel? What was it in your childhood, or in your past, that taught your body this?

DISRUPT THE IMPULSE TO APPEASE

Stop doing it.

Appeasing is a rapid movement, under threat, of our awareness away from our internal experience of distress out into the relational space between us with a focus on the Other. This is, fundamentally, a loss of clarity about what is me and what is not me.

Re-train yourself to stay with your inward experience of discomfort. Attend to its contours of feeling. Start small. Practice doing this. Practice it in low-stakes situations, with strangers. Practice it in line at the coffee shop. Practice it in places and with people you don't know.

REFOCUS ON YOUR INTERNAL EXPERIENCE

Continue to focus on your internal experience. Ask yourself—*What am I actually feeling inside?*

WORK WITH THIS DEFENSIVE STATE

If you are going into fight-flight, work with this state. (You can refer back to the earlier section in this book on working with fight-flight.)

If you are going into shutdown, work with this state. (You can refer back to the earlier section in this book on working with shutdown.)

Recognize that as you do this it will likely feel strange and un-familiar both to you, and to those you are in relationship with.

GRIEF

As you begin to change the way that you relate to conflict there is likely to be grief. Make space to allow this to arise. Let's examine for a moment why we appease. What is driving this behavior?

All of us have a fundament need for safety and for belonging. Most of us learned to appease in order to continue to get those needs met. As small children, our deepest fear is that the we will not be safe, and we will not belong– because at that devel-opmental stage we cannot take care of ourselves. We are utterly biological dependent on others. This is one of the unique attri-butes of wearing a human body. Within five minutes of being born, a colt can stand up on wobbly legs and follow its mother. But a human baby is not even fully neurologically cooked until 18 months of age. It takes us three months to learn to control our arms, and a year to learn to walk. We are biologically totally dependent on caregivers for at least this period of time.

Later in life, far beneath the surface of appeasing behaviors is a deep and often unacknowledged fear that if we stop doing this, the other person will leave. That we will be left. Abandoned. And the pain of this is so great that we are willing to abandon ourselves.

SELF-COMPASSION

It is very important to practice self-compassion when you are doing this. As you begin to shift this habit, you may find your body releasing stored memory, emotion, and other content.

Be aware that because what we are talking about here is rene-gotiating the way energy moves through us, as you move out into the world with this newfound awareness, it is going to be tested. If you begin to develop and fortify boundaries that you have not had before, the world will come up against these boundaries to test them. This is a beautiful opportunity for you to continue to practice building the muscle of changing habits. It also sucks. You will have to claw back the space that has been taken from you. Anticipate that this will happen until the new habits of boundary-setting are in place.

If you fall back into older patterns, you will know this, because you will find yourself eating other people's waste energy again, and you will feel this. Don't be hard on yourself when this happens: learning new patterns here around this stuff is not easy. Keep doing the work.

PRACTICE COMMUNICATING DIRECTLY

For many people who are in the habit of appeasing, communicating our needs directly feels uncomfortable. This is a practice. Again, it can make sense to practice communicating directly in low-stakes situations, and to learn how it feels when we do this, what kind of backlash we may face, and how to manage the arousal that is evoked when this happens.

Like doing repetitions with light weights, this practice conditions us for the energetic dynamics of moving through the world without appeasing, without apologizing for the space that we take up.

Direct communication is a vocal assertion that our needs matter. That we have a right to be here, that we have a right to take up space, that we merit consideration. At an existential level, moving though the world appeasing is a form of living apology. *Oh, I'm sorry that I exist, I'm sorry that I am taking up space. I apologize.* But you are not an accident. You came here on purpose.

In reality, none of us deserve to be here. We did not imbue

ourselves with the mysterious spark of life. The entire nature of existence is a grace. But if you are here, and you can only be reading these words if you are here, the opportunity is for you to sovereignly occupy this garment made from recycled stars that is your body. And you do honor to it by operating from clarity and humility. And this clarity and humility expresses through directness.

One of the marks of autonomic fluency is that the meaning of our words matches the energy of our words. That they are congruent. When the energetic signature matches the meaning, we can relax, and the world can relax around us, because we are saying and being what we mean.

To communicate what we see and what we need directly is a form of intelligence. And in a world of professional mendacity, a world of illusion and fabrication, of fake news and artificial intelligence and lies, being a person who communicates and embodies clarity and directness liberates you to embody your own authority.

PRACTICE: EMBODYING THE ANIMAL ENERGY OF STATES

Our everyday language is peppered with references to animals enacting autonomic states. In the face of something overwhelming, we talk about being 'frozen like a deer in headlights,' or 'playing 'possom.' We pounce on an opportunity 'like a tiger.' Like a cat our hair stands on end. Animals provide for us, almost unwittingly, a primal vocabulary of autonomic state and its accompanying gestural repertoires. If you have a dog, and you really pay attention to it, you can learn a great deal about the ANS. Our ANS is very similar to the dog's, and so watching them walk the perimeter of a new environment sniffing, turn circles and then mark before lying down, or watching their hackles rise when they hear someone getting near the house can actually teach us about our own deep nervous systems. Watching the way that they shift into sociality– here comes the tail wag– is a living demonstration about how we can shift from defense (barking) to social engagement (tailwags, licking). Watching the way that they metabolize excess arousal– my dog will shake himself violently, sometimes he will sneeze, teaches me something useful about myself.

Unlike humans, animals do not have the cortical circuitry to override autonomic impulses. We humans are, in fact, the only creatures that can suppress these signals. When we go to the vet, my dog will literally shake with fear. That's not something I generally allow myself to do, even if I am feeling that afraid. Maybe I should, because when the dog is done at the vet's, he is really done. He might be tired afterward, but he doesn't accumulate that stress and carry it home. The event doesn't traumatize him: he processes it in realtime.

One of the most astonishing things that Peter Levine, Ph.D., the developer of Somatic Experiencing[1] noticed was that animals in the wild display innate resilient responses. They will spontaneously come out of shutdown states on their own.[2] Interestingly (or tragically, I suppose) those same animals, in captivity, stop displaying these innate resilient responses. Animals in a zoo don't do them. What Levine noticed is that modern people act, in this regard, like animals in captivity. As we seek automic fluency, it can help to take a play book from the martial arts, and from ancestral storytelling cultures, and learn to mimic the movement and energy of different animals, with a particular focus on their autonomic state.

If a particular state is not available to you, is not on your menu, can you learn to explore and experience the energy of the state by mimicking an animal that does it naturally? We can learn fight responses by mimicking the stalking and predatory behavior of lions, tigers, jaguars. We can practice the bodyset of the regal jaguar, practice the grounded confidence of the way that an apex predator slings their weight through the world. We can learn flight responses by mimicking the evasive actions of prey animals like deer and gazelles. We can practice the alertness with which the deer's ears prick up while eating, the way that they swivel, listening as it chews, scanning the surroundings, and the way that they can instantaneously bolt into action if coyote springs out of the underbrush.

---

1   Somatic Experiencing is a naturalistic approach to the resolution of trauma.

2   Gazelle's LUCKY ESCAPE from CHEETAH and HYENA by PLAYING DEAD!
https://www.youtube.com/watch?v=Lupt2qajcJg

25- YOU'RE GOING THE WRONG WAY

I know a lot of people who fight with their Autonomic Nervous Systems. Their bodies know something, but their heads don't know how they know it, and rather than simply listening to what the body is telling them, they start to argue with it. Sometimes you can see this on someone's face.

I don't like the word intuition because I think it is lazy. Intuition just means that we know something and we don't know how we know it. I find this lazy because the body has myriad ways of knowing that are non-cognitive, and I want to encourage us to figure out where these knowings are coming from. In our brain-centric world, we don't know whether knowings are coming from our guts, or our hands, or our feet, or our genitals, or an inward voice, or the trees whispering something in our ears, or the auguries and omens of the more-than-human world. I want us to get curious about this rather than simply lumping it all into a single category.

I want the non-cognitive ways of knowing of our bodies to become signals that we can rely on. The next time you find yourself knowing something, but don't know how you know it, try listening to it and see what happens. I'm not talking about major life decisions, necessarily. I might be talking about just turning toward or away from someone in the street, or leaving a meeting because suddenly something doesn't feel right to you, even though you don't understand why. I'm talking about respecting that the innate and sovereign knowings of your body, if you start to act upon them, could become a novel and reliable way of navigating through the world. That they could assemble into some coherent mode of sense-making.

During the pandemic I was truly astonished by how many people I saw making decisions that showed me that they did not understand where their wellbeing was coming from. I'm going to share a little secret with you. It's a secret that I just wrote

a 552 page book about, so I guess that really its neither little, nor is it a secret.[11] Your wellbeing comes from experiencing connection to yourself, others, and the Living and More-than-Human worlds. If you want to feel well, get yourself operating from a baseline in safety and connection in 51% of your present moments. This is essentially the algorithm for wellness.

Connection is the deepest form of nourishment for your ANS. At a neurological level, what I'm talking about is creating enough of a felt sense of safety that your snail can come out of its shell into the world, and you can become relationally available. Of course, availability is more vulnerable– and we live in an extraction engine, more or less, so this vulnerability is uncomfortable for many of us because it is often exploited. But you know what? It is where your life awaits. From the stand-point of your ANS, each moment of connection is food. You would not forget to eat for a week, but I know many people who forget to feed themselves connection on the regular. This became really apparent to me during the pandemic, when suddenly in mid-March of 2020, when the world went into lock-down, all of the ordinary micro-moments of connection were collectively snatched away from us. We take a lot of things for granted. Most of us do not really appreciate the air that we breathe until particulate matter from a wildfire makes inhaling sting our lungs. Or the water we drink until we find ourselves in a desert without it. I didn't really appreciate the potency of connection in nourishing us until COVID-19 robbed it from us overnight.

With masks preventing us from seeing the social cues on one another's faces, and six feet of distance keeping us from touching one another, all of the micro-moments of interaction– the taps on the arm, the tugs on the shirt, the exchange of smiles, high-fives, and hugs dwindled away to zero. No more tiny head nods from a distance. No more knowing glances, secret smiles– our faces were replaced by blank masks. Deprived of touch

1 *The Neurobiology of Connection: Re-Wilding your Deep Nervous System for Welbeing* by Natureza Gabriel

and the ability to see one another's faces, our nervous systems collectively shifted, at first gradually, and then precipitously, in the direction of threat. There was a lockdown in most countries of the world, but we have underestimated the degree to which this lockdown was internalized as well. For many people, that pandemic has not truly ended. In its wake is the shadow pandemic of loneliness, isolation, and disconnection.

If you can't hug your friends, smile with strangers, tap someone on the shoulder when they drop something- you lose this flow of micro-moments of connection that had been buoying many of us along on an invisible thread of relating. And in its absence, where do you get your connection needs met? This was a time that I really turned to the forest, spending more and more of my days out-of-doors, in nature, communing with trees, birds, plants, and animals. I did this as a sort of innate survival mechanism. I knew I needed to get my hands deep in the dirt, to hold on to the earth, to preserve my relating with other beings if humans were not available to me.

Yet I also learned so much about the many portals to the Connection System. How we can connect through face and voice, through touch- this I already knew. But I learned about connecting through the feet, through the skin, through song. I learned about connecting through gesture, through posture, through balance. Through rhythm, through gravity, through language. Through craft. Through movement.

And I sought out a steady diet of connection, foraged from alternate sources, since the many friendships I had cultivated before the pandemic were not available to me. I sought out relating with beings I might not have ordinarily noticed had the world not been interrupted. I grew my relating with a number of trees. A family of squirrels. A watershed. A mycelial network. A place. I foraged and wild-crafted connection nourishment because I could no longer find it in the places I had before.

WHERE WILL YOU SOURCE YOUR CONNECTION NOURISHMENT?

My point here is that if we understand deeply enough that connection is the ground of wellbeing, we can find ways to access it even when the ordinary routes we might take are not an option. Just because the places we have ordinarily, or historically sought connection are not available, does not mean that we cannot seek out the nourishment of connection.

Where do you find your connection nourishment? In what corners of your life, waiting to nourish you, are the attributes of connection? And how might you organize your life differently, how might you change your priorities, if you realized that those were keys to unlocking your wellbeing?

26- WRAPPING UP

In this brief volume I have attempted to help you build an understanding of what your Autonomic Nervous System is, how it works, why it is so important to your moment-to-moment experience of wellbeing, and how to begin navigating signals it is sending you through how you feel.

This process of building first awareness, then fluency, and then agency is one that my colleague Sue Bahnan first recognized as a sequence. We have to understand how these systems work and begin to feel them to begin to use them to navigate to begin to leverage them to transform our lives.

My hope is that this fractal process (awareness, fluency, agency) becomes a spiraling that can organize for your journey into self-knowledge through an autonomic lens, and that as you learn this primal ancestral language of awareness it fortifies your wellbeing, your sense of kinship with all the other lifeforms that communicate autonomically, and your deepening groundedness and embodiment. Your autonomic nervous system, once you come into relationship with it, is the deepest compass you have for orienting your life.

I'd like to conclude with some additional questions for reflection. The point of these is not to get answers down on the page– this isn't an exam– it is to help you abide in generative questions.

QUESTIONS FOR REFLECTION

How does your body communicate with you non-cognitively?

What parts of your body reliably send you signals that you sometimes ignore but that seem like they might be meaningful?

Is there any part of your body that seems like it has something to tell you regularly?

How might you increase your ability to listen to these signals from the body, that often show up as unusual sensations, discomfort, or even pain?

What would happen if you began to interpret all of your sensations as meaningful?

What if even pain was meaningful?

Given that connection is a form of nourishment that you require, where do you source connection?

What practices of connection might it be useful to you to strengthen?

What things do you notice that you are doing when you are thriving that you might not do when you do not feel as well? For example– often when I am feeling great I have the spontaneous desire to dance. When I'm feeling great this just happens, but probably dancing makes me feel great at other times as well. I might be well advised to do it more.

What are the most important things that you learned about the ANS from this book?

What is one thing that you want to put into practice in your life as a result of learning about the ANS?

Thanks for learning with me!

I hope that this time has served you well.

-Gabriel

THE AUTONOMIC COMPASS

QUITE POSSIBLY
THE WORLD'S MOST SOPHISTICATED SELF-HEALING PLATFORM

- ASSESS AUTONOMIC LANDSCAPE WITH TAILORED DIAGNOSTICS
- TAILOR PRACTICES TO MEET NEEDS OF YOUR NERVOUS SYSTEM
- HUNDREDS OF PRACTICES, DOZENS OF EDUCATIONAL FILMS
- TEACHERS FROM AROUND THE WORLD

This work feels like a foundational piece of wellness and overall health that I feel has long been missing from the medical conversation. I love how it is based in the science of how we function– it is very practical, very direct. I've witnessed its effectiveness with my patients. These are places that I don't think traditional medicine or mental health has succeeded in reaching, and I find this work extremely inspiring and hopeful in its implications for healing.

–Nadine Burke Harris MD MPH, Former First Surgeon General of California

http://hearthscience.io/autonomic-compass

THE NEUROBIOLOGY OF CONNECTION
RE-WILDING YOUR DEEP NERVOUS SYSTEM FOR WELLBEING

In this tour-de-force from ancestral neuroscience pioneer Natureza Gabriel, the developer of Autonomics, learn to grasp and move the deepest and most powerful levers that govern your moment-to-moment experience of wellbeing.

Learn how safety turns on the neurobiology of connection, connection activates grounded interoception, interoception births intuition, intuition sparks relatedness, and relatedness activates enduring wellbeing.

http://hearthscience.io

Natureza Gabriel (aka Gabriel Kram) is the principal neural architect of *Autonomics*, a cutting-edge & ancestral update to our understanding of living autonomic physiology, which he has developed over 30 years of trans-disciplinary study and research with input from well over 5,000 wellness professionals, and 100 mentors and advisors from 25 lineages of healing in 24 cultures. His mind was trained at Yale and Stanford Universities, his heart has been educated in ceremonies and circles. He has spent 30 years studying connection through the lenses of neuroscience, mindful awareness, social justice, deep nature connection, non-cognitive ways of knowing, Indigenous Lifeways, and cultural linguistics.

He is Founder and CEO of Hearth Science: a translation research firm pioneering the union of neurophysiology and ancestral awareness to turn on the deepest drivers of human wellbeing. He is the principal architect of the Autonomic Compass, a proprietary diagnostics and treatment software platform that centralizes autonomic physiology in the diagnosis and treatment of stress-related disorders and the creation of enduring wellbing. He is Host and Executive Producer of *The Restorative Practices Film Series, The Connection Masterclass, Evoking Connection States*, and *Lectures on the New Foundation Model in Autonomics*. In autumn 2023 has was asked to lead the global Polyvagal Study Group on Facebook. He has been asked to teach Autonomics to people in 50 countries, executives in Fortune 500 companies, the faculty of medical schools, governments, international NGOs, and tribal leaders. He is the author of the *Connection Phenomenology Series.* This is his twelfth book.

He lives with his family on unceded Miwok territory (Bay Area) in South Salmon Nation (California) on western Turtle Island (United States). You can find more of his work, as well as that of the extraordinary faculty of Hearth Science at

HTTP://www.hearthscience.io